P. Demarest Johnson

Claudius, the Cowboy of Ramapo Valley

A Story of revolutionary Times in southern New York

P. Demarest Johnson

Claudius, the Cowboy of Ramapo Valley
A Story of revolutionary Times in southern New York

ISBN/EAN: 9783743324657

Manufactured in Europe, USA, Canada, Australia, Japa

Cover: Foto ©ninafisch / pixelio.de

Manufactured and distributed by brebook publishing software (www.brebook.com)

P. Demarest Johnson

Claudius, the Cowboy of Ramapo Valley

CLAUDIUS,

The Cowboy of Ramapo Valley.

A Story of Revolutionary Times in Southern New York.

—BY—

P. DEMAREST JOHNSON

MIDDLETOWN, N. Y.:
SLAUSON & BOYD, PRESS STEAM PRINT.
1894.

Entered according to Act of Congress, in the year one thousand eight hundred and ninety-four,

BY P. DEMAREST JOHNSON,

In the office of the Librarian of Congress, at Washington.

Dedication.

TO

GEORGE W. SUFFERN,

MY LONG TIME FRIEND AND A DESCENDANT OF ONE OF THE STAUNCHEST PATRIOTS OF THE TIME THAT TRIED MEN'S SOULS, AND IN REMEMBRANCE OF THE MANY HAPPY HOURS WE HAVE PASSED TOGETHER IN RAMBLING AMONG THE RUGGED MOUNTAINS AND THROUGH THE HISTORIC VALLEYS OF OUR BIRTH PLACE,

THIS LITTLE BOOK IS DEDICATED,

WITH THE HOPE THAT MANY MORE OF THOSE PLEASANT HOURS MAY INTERVENE BEFORE OUR PATHS SHALL SEPARATE.

THE AUTHOR.

PREFACE.

The part of the country where the scenes of this story are mainly laid is certainly one of the most romantic and beautiful in the land. Between what has always been designated as The Point of the Mountain and the Highlands of the Hudson near the present village of Nyack, lie the rolling lands comprising the county of Rockland. For splendid and romantic scenery it will compare favorably with any county in the State. Not many New Yorkers know what a little Switzerland there is so near the great city or what rugged mountains and pleasant valleys are to be found almost at their doors and how little need there is, to travel to the distant Adirondacks, to find sparkling streams, limpid lakes, and the other handiwork of nature which makes that region so attractive to the seeker of pleasure.

But not only for these things is this portion of the State remarkable. Among its rugged peaks and gently rolling hills may be found relics of the time that tried men's souls; and many a place can be pointed out to the wayfarer, which has been hallowed and made sacred by the presence of the great hero of human freedom and the men who followed him in that long, and finally victorious struggle.

To the patriotic citizen, and one who loves to ramble among such scenes, many days of pleasure, and profit too, await him, if he will put himself into the hands of some old pioneer acquainted with this stretch of country and be shown where, in the dark days of the revolution, those men of iron stood on guard amid the rocks and ravines of historic Ramapo Pass.

As to the characters in this little story: many of them were the true actors in the drama then being enacted and were living men and women of the time. Claudius is so much a true character, that still, among the oldest inhabitants of that district, he is known as the Scourge of the Highlands and the tradition of his desperate and cruel deeds has been handed down from father to son; and in the literature of the two counties of Orange and Rockland, he has a prominent place.

Rem. Onderdonk too, was more of a hero than he is pictured here, and was really a daring and impetuous scout throughout the whole conflict; and his memory is still fresh and green among the descendants of that family which has always occupied a prominent position in that part of the State.

Many of the incidents here related are also matters of fact and well known among the old families whose forefathers were the first settlers and pioneers of the old county of Orange; and thus may be seen that the whole story, though colored somewhat by the imagination of the author, has a basis of fact and truth, and in many instances, does not exaggerate what transpired there when the yeoman of Orange helped strike the blow for liberty whose reverberations were heard around the world.

THE AUTHOR.

CLAUDIUS,

THE COWBOY OF RAMAPO VALLEY.

CHAPTER I.

"For my own part I do not believe the King and Parliament have the right to tax tea, or, for that matter, any other commodity imported by us ; and if this business is persisted in it will lead to bloodshed and it may be revolution outright. The times are wild and unsettled and I shall prepare myself for the worst and be ready to act my part in what may prove to be a bloody drama."

"I do not agree with you, Barent. I believe the government has the right to tax its subjects for the good of the nation, and though I think it will never come to such a serious pass as you imagine, if it should, I give you my word that I shall always be found upon the side of my King fighting against the traitorous faction which has for years already spoken lightly of his authority and been breeding contempt for the laws of the land."

This was part of a conversation which occurred between two young men who had accidently met, while hunting near the base of the mountain range which constitutes the western border of what is now the county of Rockland in the Empire State of New York. The time was the autumn of 1774, just after the meeting in Philadelphia of the first General Congress and the year after the destruction of the tea in Boston harbor. The one addressed as Barent was a young man of about twenty-two years, a representative of one of the leading families of that part of the country, (the Van Houtens). The other one was a youth of probably twenty, who answered to the name of Claudius Smith. He was born among the monntains that gird the valley of the Ramapo and from boyhood had been a wild and wayward lad. His family owned a large track of mountain land, which in the eyes of the surrounding neighbors raised it above the common herd.

The young men, after some further conversation of a desultory nature, parted and took the mountainous path to their respective homes.

Barent Van Houten, as his name indicates, was a descendant of the early Dutch settlers of what was then the County of Orange in the Province of New York. His education was the best the country afforded at the time, and it was only within the last year that he had returned from the city of New York, after graduating from one of its best schools, and now, like many more of the prominent young men of the Province, felt seriously interested in the troubles which had been brewing for several years between Great Britain and her American Colonies. As is well known, the descendants of the Dutch settlers in this part of the Province of New York, were in the main found upon the patriotic side during the Revolutionary struggle, and the Van Houtons were no exception to the rule. Barent, being one of the most prominent of the young men of that family, was looked upon and recognized as a leader in all things social or political, and his influence among them was great and powerful. In person he was the perfection of manly beauty, being rather above the medium height, broad shouldered and powerfully built, with a high and expansive forehead, around which his dark hair clustered in short and wavy curls. His whole contour reminded one of a finished Corinthian column carved by the inspired hand of Phidias. The Van Honton homestead was situated in a beautiful valley near the center of what was called in those days Orange County south of the mountains. It was a typical Dutch mansion, built in the most substantial manner of stone, with hipped roof and an expansive hall running through the center from front to rear. Everything about it betokened the easy circumstances and comparative opulence of its owner. The barns and outbuildings were numerous and extensive, as was required by the large and productive farm surrounding them. The family consisted of Rulof, the father, his wife and Barent, their only child.

Among the neighbors of the Van Houtons was the large and prosperous family of the Onderdonks, distantly related, and of the same patriotic impulses. Of all the young men of the surrounding country, there was none of more earnest patriotism than Rembrandt Onderdonk, the eldest son of old Martinus, the owner of many a broad acre of smiling meadow land and forest. Rem., as he was called by his family and intimate friends, was of that wild and impulsive nature that does with the whole heart whatever is to be done without fear or ever stopping to count the cost. He was large of frame and strong of muscle, standing six feet four in his stockings, erect and powerful as the sturdy oak of his native forests, but withal of a jovial, good nature, unless excited by strong provocation, when nothing could withstand the fury of his rage. Such were the characteristics and description of Rem. Onderdonk, who, before the revolutionary struggle ended, became known throughout the district as the fighting scout of Ramapo. The family besides Rem., were Dirck, a younger son, and Katherine, the only daughter, the life of the household.

As time passed things began to take a warlike turn, and early in 1775 the news of the battle of Lexington was heralded over the land, and caused the most intense excitement. At every public place in the country and on every street corner in the cities the people were to be seen discussing the question of resistance to the demands of the mother country.

In that portion of the country where the scenes of our story are laid, the people ranged themselves either upon the patriotic, or, (as it was called in derision), the tory side of the question. In some few instances families were divided on the subject, but the great majority espoused the cause of the Colonies, and immediately set about making preparations to meet any emergency that might arise.

In 1774, at the house of Yost Mabie, at Tappan, the county seat of Orange, a Declaration of Rights had already been signed and given to the world by the leading inhabitants, setting forth in almost identical language with the preamble of the Declaration of Independence what the people demanded. Thus may be seen the spirit which animated the inhabitants and made them steadfast through more than eight long years of blood and carnage, and which in the end caused them to triumph over Great Britain's veteran soldiery.

CHAPTER II.

In one of the wildest and most secluded nooks of Ramapo Pass was gathered in the early spring of 1776 a band of young men. They were dressed, at least most of them, in backwoods or hunter costume, and all of them were armed with rifles. In the centre of the group stood one who was rather better dressed and whose rifle was more elaborately inlaid with silver and mother of pearl, and his form towered above the others like a stately pine among the humbler hemlocks of the forest. His companions stood around him in rapt attention, and it was easy to discern that they looked upon him as their leader, and one whose commands they were ready to obey. This was Claudius Smith, the tory leader of a reckless band of mountaineers, raised by him from among the fortresses of the Ramapo range, and to whom the reader had a slight introduction at the beginning of our story.

"Boys," said he, addressing those around him, "we are just now on the eve of troublous times, and I have no doubt we shall have a long and bloody war with the traitorous scoundrels who have taken up arms against our lawful King, and it now behooves us, who have always been loyal to him, to foil their designs in every way in our power. And while thus engaged, we can at the same time look out for ourselves and act upon the old maxim that 'charity begins at home.' As you all are aware, that body of traitors, these self-styled patriots called the General Congress, have passed an act and appropriated money to fortify this pass, and, in fact, have already begun the work below Sidman's Bridge. We shall, therefore, be forced to do things quietly and hide our intentions as much as possible from the argus eyes of the scouting parties who almost daily patrol this valley, which, as you know, leads into the interior of the Province. And now, comrades, let us disperse for the present, with the understanding that one week from to-day, at this same hour, we are to meet at the old cavern on the mountains, where we can lay our plans with less fear of interruption. Do not fail to be there, for by that time we shall have something of importance to claim our attention."

As the tory leader finished his short address each man shouldered his rifle and disappeared amid the gloom of the surrounding forest.

"Ha! ha! ha! O, how smart you tink you is, Mas' Claud!" And as the last of the tory gang disappeared in the darkness, there peered out from a dense laurel bush within twenty feet of their trysting place a black head, followed by the stalwart form of a negro. As he emerged from the bush he jumped up and struck his heels together three times, and as a proper ending of the performance, gave three or four steps of a plantation jig.

"O! I got you dis time, Mas' Claud. I was mos' sure you was up to some debilment! Dem tories am jist like dogs! Whar you see tree or four makin' a bizness runnin' togeder, you kin be mos' sartin dat somebody's sheep am gwine to suffer. Now I'se bound to sarcumvent your debiltry sure." And saying this, Black George, as he was known the country over, grasped his rifle and struck a bee line for the residence of old Martinus Onderdonk, where he had resided all his life, and to whom both himself and parents belonged as slaves.

It was quite late in the evening when George reached the Onderdonk mansion, but he found Rembrandt and several of the young Whigs of the neighborhood, among them being Barent Van Houton, in close and earnest consultation. Before the negro had reached the house he saw the light flickering through one of the shutters, and came to the conclusion that before going to bed, he must inform Mas' Rem. what he had overheard while lying concealed in the laurel bush. He, therefore, tapped at the window through which he saw the light. In a moment Rem. appeared, and recognizing George, immediately asked what was wanted. The negro whispered into his ear that he had something of importance to communicate. Without further ado Rem. led George in the midst of the assembled company and told him to unfold his secret before them all. George told them all he had heard and seen at the secret meeting of the tory band ; how young Claudius Smith had addressed them and seemed to be their leader, and, finally, of the projected gathering of the band a week hence at the cavern on the mountain.

This, of course, was news to the assembled young men, and though some of them had suspicions as to the patriotism of Claudius, still they had not thought he would take an active part against the majority of his countrymen. But now they were undeceived, for they well knew the truthfulness and honesty of Black George, and they were sure he had given them a correct report of what he had discovered.

After George had told his story, the young men held a sort of council of war. Barent Van Honten, who, as was noted before, composed one of the number who had met by appointment at the Onderdonk homestead, immediately suggested that it would be wise to closely watch Claudius and his future movements and if he committed any overt act, to report it at once to the military headquarters at Tappan. He also announced that a company had been organized there and were asking for recruits to fill up its ranks. "Now is the time," said he, "to show our patriotism by our acts, and setting the example to others by enlisting in the service of the country, and I feel sure there is not one present but feels the same as I do and is ready to throw his all into the scales and abide by the issue, whatever that may be."

This little speech had the desired effect, for one and all announced their intention of enlisting in the ranks of the patriot army which was being organized throughout the land.

Thus it may be observed how the seeds of liberty planted by the sturdy fathers of our land germinated in after years and produced a crop of patriotic martyrs whose blood enriched the soil of freedom and in the end built up the mighty fabric whose blessings we now enjoy. It was a late hour when the party dispersed, each one with the full intention of carrying into effect the resolution made at the meeting.

The next day Rem. Onderdonk made his way to the house of his intimate friend Barent, and, together, they proceeded to Tappan, the headquarters of the company which was being organized for the service. Barent had already been elected a lieutenant in the company and was, therefore, in a hurry to reach the place.

Rem.'s intention in going there was to obtain through the assistance of Barent a commission as captain of scouts and to receive permission from the committee of safety to raise a company whose business should be to patrol the west bank of the Hudson and watch the movements of the predatory bands of tories and cowboys which infested the country lying between that river and Ramapo Pass. His mission proved successful and he proceeded immediately to raise his company, which was accomplished in a very short time, when he announced himself ready to begin operations.

To say that Rem. was in his glory at the prospect of being instrumental in circumventing the royalists did not fully express his feelings on this occasion. His company consisted of young and sturdy patriots whose souls were in the cause and whose confidence in their leader was supreme. Leaving Captain Rem. in a business so much in harmony with his impulsive nature, we will take the reader to somewhat different scenes.

CHAPTER III.

On the broad piazza of a large and comfortable looking dwelling situated among the pleasant surroundings of rural life, and on the highway leading from Ramapo Pass, were seated, in the early evening of a beautiful day in 1776, a young couple in earnest conversation.

"My dear Mary," said the young man to his companion, "the time has arrived when every young man should feel himself in duty bound to aid his struggling country in the effort she is now making to free herself from the oppression of Great Britain. She needs the influence and material aid of all her sons and daughters too. I am well aware of the tremendous and unequal struggle before us, but with an honest belief in the justice of her cause, and a firm reliance on Him who always fights the battles of the weak, I am confident that we will triumph in the end"

"I believe as you do, Barent, but to think of

all the misery that such a war will bring upon our land almost unnerves me," said his companion.

The reader, of course, recognizes the young man as Barent Van Houten, and we will introduce his companion as Mary Demaray, the only child of old Bernhard Demaray, the most prominent representative of the Huguenot family of that name in the Province. She was beautiful beyond most of her sex. Her hair hung in dark tresses to her slender waist; her eyes were large and black and of that peculiar expression which tells of love unquenchable, and firm reliance and faith in the object of her affections. Mary Demaray was not the plaything of an hour, nor the kind of young woman that needs to be placed in a hot house atmosphere for fear of withering, but one of the kind born for something higher and better and whose nature was calculated to strengthen and sustain the object to which it clung.

"What you say is no doubt too true," rejoined Barent. "Misery and suffering are the accompaniments of every war, but the die is cast and the Congress in session at Philadelphia issued a Declaration of Independence on the 4th day of last July. It only remains for every true lover of his country to use his earnest endeavor to sustain and uphold that declaration."

"Yes," said she, "and I would not have you do otherwise, dear Barent; for I too, though only a woman, have noted each successive act of oppression passed by the Parliament and consented to by the King, as if for the purpose of driving us to rebellion and, I suppose, if we should remain passive under these, others of a more virulent nature would be heaped upon us."

"But the worst feature of this business," continued Barent, "is that there are some persons and families of influence among us who not only feel coldly toward our cause, but, I fear, will even take up arms against us under pretense of loyalty to the King. They are being closely watched and we hope to frustrate their evil designs; but they can certainly do us much harm and may cause this war to assume a more horrid front by their unnatural behavior. However, let us hope for better days and more peaceful times."

Barent took an affectionate leave of his betrothed, sprung into the saddle and was away to his company at Tappan. Mary watched her lover until his form was lost in the dim twilight, when she turned and entered the house. where her father, the staunch old Whig, was sitting.

"Well, Mary! what good news did Barent bring?" asked the old man. "Nothing of greater import than that the Congress now in session at Philadelphia almost unanimously issued a Declaration of Independence on the 4th day of last July," replied the daughter.

"Well done for them! I glory in their staunch patriotism. The world will now know what we are fighting for! There is nothing indefinite about that, and it will cause the line to be strictly drawn between patriot and traitor so that we shall know who are our friends, and who our foes."

Although the Declaration of Independence had been signed several months previously, Barent had brought the first news of the event to this retired spot, the delay of course being due to the lack of telegraphs and railroads at the time of which we are writing. This important event gave hope and courage to the Whigs and caused depresssion and anger among the tories throughout the land.

CHAPTER IV.

About a week after the meeting of the young Whigs at the house of Rem. Onderdonk, himself and Black George might have been seen in earnest consultation near one of the large Dutch barns at the rear of the dwelling. "Now George," said Rem., "I shall depend upon you to find out exactly where the meeting place of these tories is situated. Where that cavern is located, I do not certainly know, but I feel sure that you can find it and therefore I want you to start this afternoon, as to-night you know is the time set for their meeting. Proceed to the foot of the mountain, conceal yourself at some point where you can see without yourself being seen, and I am almost confident you will notice some of them on their way there, when you can stealthily follow, keeping yourself out of sight, and finally locate the headquarters of the gang."

"I am de boy for dat bizness, Mas' Rem!" said

George. "Jist you leab it to me, and if I don't run dem tories to dar hole, you kin call me a fool nigger!"

This was a business which exactly suited Black George, and he began the work immediately. Going into the large, old-fashioned kitchen he took from its resting place his trusty old rifle, and taking a path that led through the heavy woodland northward, he was soon lost to view from the farm house. Striking across the dense swamps and forests which lay between the Onderdonk farm and the base of Kakiatt mountain, he was soon upon ground where he deemed concealment to be the better part of valor. He consequently kept himself under cover as much as possible, picking his way through the underbrush, which grew on the mountain side. He finally secreted himself in an almost impenetrable thicket on one of the foot hills of the range.

"Now den, Mas' Claud! I is in dis nest fer to watch yer capers, an' if dis child don't find out where ye put up nights, den my name ain't George," said the negro to himself.

He had not been secreted more than half an

hour when he heard a cautious footstep below him. Peeping cautiously from the bush in which he had taken refuge, George saw a man with his rifle slung across his shoulder slowly and carefully ascending the hill. He passed within a dozen yards of where the negro lay and made his way silently toward the summit. He had scarcely gone a hundred yards when George emerged from his hiding place and quietly followed him.

"Dis am a hot trail sure, and I'se got de scent strong, and I guess I won't lose it," said George to himself, as he stepped quietly along behind the man. They kept on in this way for some time until the person in advance had nearly reached the summit, when he suddenly stopped and gave a peculiar whistle, low and somewhat prolonged. In a moment it was answered from what seemed a rift in the rocks to the left of where he stood. Again another low, short note and an answering one from the rocks and then a man appeared as though he had risen out of the earth close beside the rift. The man then advanced and the two disappeared as though by magic. Black George lay low now, and from then until darknes closed in around the mountain, he saw eighteen armed men approach, give the signal, and disappear in the rift in the rocks. The negro now marked well the lay of the land, noted the different land marks, and feeling sure he would have no trouble in locating the cavern afterwards, carefully descended the mountain and before midnight was again at the Onderdonk homestead. He immediately communicated what he had discovered to Mas' Rem., who, after questioning him to his satisfaction, told him to be sure to keep in mind the direction and landmarks by which to locate the cavern, as his knowledge would, in the near future, be put to the test. "All right, Mas' Rem, I got 'em all here," and Black George tapped his forehead significantly, to show where he had stored the knowledge.

Among the many admirers of Katharine Onderdonk, the beautiful and accomplished daughter of old Martinus, was young Claudius Smith, the suspected leader of the tory band. He had been quite a frequent visitor at the mansion in the past, and from appearances an not altogether unwelcome one—at least so thought several of the young men who had some aspirations to the hand of Katherine—and so his appearance there three days after George had located the tory headquarters on the mountain did not seem a thing unusual to the casual observer.

Claudius was received by Katharine in a cordial manner and invited into the dwelling. His horse was taken by one of the colored servants and properly cared for, and everything was done to make his visit as agreeable as possible. But he did not seem to feel at ease, and Katharine noticed during the conversation that he was preoccupied and his whole demeanor like one who had something weighty on his mind. In the evening Rem. arrived at home and was met by George, who immediately imformed him of the presence of Claudius in the house. A frown spread over Rem.'s usually pleasant countenance, and after inquiring of George how long he had been there strode into the room where his sister was entertaining her visitor.

"Good evening Claudius!" said Rem. as he entered. "Good evening Rembrandt!" returned Claudius. "The weather is fine and the air bracing, and I enjoyed my ride over here more than I can tell you." "Yes," said Rem., "the weather is fine and everything in nature looks favorable, but our country is entering upon what may prove a long and bloody struggle against the tyranny of a mad King and what appears to be an insane Parliament."

"Well," remarked Claudius, "as to there being a long war, it may be true, but as to the tyranny of the King and Parliament, I believe their acts are legal, and that it is only right and proper that we should assist in paying for our own protection. The armies of the mother country were sent here to aid us in defending our soil against the invasion of the French and the atrocities of their savage allies ; and now, when she needs our help financially, I see no reason in our resisting her just demands."

"I had hoped for better things from you, Claudius," returned Rem., "and imagined that in you we would have a strong, intelligent and faithful ally ; but it seems I have been deceived in so thinking, and must, though reluctantly, place you among the enemies of Liberty."

"If to be loyal to our annointed King, and

ready to uphold the laws of the land, makes one an enemy to liberty, you are welcome to place me in that category," replied Claudius.

Katharine, who had been sitting by silently thus far, now made an effort to turn the conversation toward a less dangerous subject. She therefore inquired of Rem. (who had just returned from the neighborhood of King's Ferry), as to the health of some relatives residing there. But he did not seem to hear her, and said to Claudius :

"Well, we have been friends for many years, and I had hoped to remain such for many more ; but the time has arrived when we must consider those who are not for us as being against us."

"As to that, you must use your own judgment ; but let me warn you, Rembrandt, to beware of following the lead of the traitorous crew who, as I am informed, are already organizing an army to withstand the just demands of the mother country, for it will bring swift destruction upon the head of every one found in the ranks, and in open treason to the government," said Claudius, as Rem. bade him goodbye and left the house.

He remained but a short time at the Onderdonk

mansion after his rather exciting conversation with Rem., and which had left a bitter feeling in the hearts of the young men. Of course his opinions found no sympathy in that quarter, and even Katharine concluded that the principles held by Claudius were not calculated to promote good feeling in that community ; and she really hoped his visits there might become less frequent.

CHAPTER V.

Ramapo Valley, which pierces, and really cuts in twain, the rugged hills of the Ramapo range, is one of the most remarkable defiles in the country. The scenery throughout the entire sixteen miles of its length is grand and imposing. At no place is it more than half a mile in width. From the narrow pass at its southern outlet, where stand the twin peaks of Noorde Kup, and Hooghe Kup, to its northern extremity, where the mountains slope down into the fertile fields of old Orange, it is romantic beyond description. Upon either side rise the rugged granite walls, from a thousand to fifteen hundred feet in height, while through the center of the valley flow the waters of the lovely Ramapo river; here, gliding peacefully along through smiling meadows, and again, leaping in mad energy over scraggy rocks, or tumbling in mist and foam over miniature Niagaras, making it all in all one of the most delightful mountain valleys in this broad land.

At the time of which we write it was closely settled. Near the southern mouth, fortifications in the shape of a couple of block houses had been erected at some previous period for protection against the Indians, and near by them was a single farm house. From there northward through the valley was here and there a farm house or a log hut of a mountaineer, until you came near the northern end, where a more imposing structure had been built. It was a substantial log house of considerable size and stood in a sheltered nook of the mountains on the east side of the valley. Its surroundings were such as betokened easy circumstances in those who occupied it. The outbuildings were extensive and in good repair, and everything about indicated that the lord of this mansion was not of the common herd.

This was the home of the Smith family, of which Claudius was a prominent member. The family consisted of the old man Jacobus, his wife Maria, both of whom had already passed the common limit of three score years and ten; two sons, Cobus and Claudius; and a daughter named Sally.

The whole family was noted for the size and strength of its members ; for their rugged endurance, and above all for a certain shrewdness in making bargains ; in fact for knowing how to make money, and keeping it after it was made. But above all the rest, were these characteristics developed in the youngest son, Claudius. Not only was he the giant of the family physically, but also far above them in intellect, and all that goes to make a leader of men ; but as the reader has had an introduction to him before, we need follow this line no farther. Be it known from henceforth, that he was *the* Smith of the family, and the one who afterwards made the name known throughout the land ; whether for good or evil, the reader may be able to decide when our story is told.

It was quite late in the evening when Claudius returned from his visit to Katharine Onderdonk, and as might be expected he was not in the best humor, for he clearly saw that under the circumstances it was doubtful whether his suit for the hand of the patriotic maiden would prove successful. He feared the influence of Rem. on his sister would prove too heavy a factor to be eliminated even by the love he thought the daughter of old Martinus bore him. As he arrived at the house he threw himself from the saddle and entered the room where his mother and sister were sitting engaged in some feminine occupation.

A mother's eye, it is said, can discern the workings of her offspring's heart quicker and truer than all the world beside. The mother of Claudius was no exception to the rule, for he had scarcely set his feet across the threshold when the old lady discovered the cloud on his brow.

"How now Claud!" said she, "what is it ails my boy? "What has come over you that I see the bad light in your eye?" "Nothing, mother, that amounts to anything excepting that there are many more traitors to the King than I or any one else expected." "Ah, my boy, it is more than that worries you! Has old Onderdonk's daughter jilted you? If she has it serves you right, and shame it is that a son of ours should be currying favors from such as they," replied the old woman.

Such talk from his mother still further angered Claudius, as he answered: "No mother you are wide of the mark. It is not love, but war that I am thinking of. Instead of Cupid with his boyish pranks and harmless weapons it will be old Mars, the horrid god of war, at whose shrine we will all be worshipping ; for as I live, I believe ere the new year comes around the war cry will be heard ringing among the hills and valleys of our land. The whole country seems ripe for rebellion, and it behooves us, who are friends of the King, to make preparation to aid him in crushing out the spirit of revolt, which is stalking ghostlike over the whole country."

"Where is Cobus?" asked Claudius of his mother. "I do not know, though he was here a short time ago. He may be at neighbor Jones'," answered the old lady.

Cobus was the eldest of the two brothers, in whom Claudius placed great confidence and whose counsel he sought on all occasions. Leaving his mother and sister, he started in search of his brother whom he found at the barn, having just returned from a short visit to one of the neighbors. They held long counsel together, the purport of which is made known by the parting words of

Claudius: "See every man if possible by tomorrow night. Inform them where we are to meet, and do not forget to impress upon them the fact that there may be work to do, and therefore to come thoroughly armed and ready for active service." "I will see that all is done as you require," replied Cobus.

With these words the brothers parted and retired to their respective couches to woo the drowsy god of sleep.

CHAPTER VI.

On the 17th of June, 1775, the battle of Bunker Hill occurred and the particulars thereof were sent to every nook and corner of the Provinces. It was the first time, really, that any considerable number of the opposing forces had been engaged, and the result was such as to encourage the patriotic sons of America to nobler and more effective efforts. It had been discovered that American militiamen were able to meet the veteran soldiers of Great Britain, and, on even terms to at least hold their own, and render a good account of themselves. Only for the reason that ammunition had failed, they would probably have destroyed the greater portion of the army that was sent to dislodge them.

This opening battle of the Revolution was condusive of much good to the patriotic cause. It infused new life into the hearts of the people, and in fact caused the whole country to spring to arms. From the bleak hills of New Hampshire to the smiling savannas of our southern land, the call to arms was heard. It united and consolidated the different Provinces in the bold determination to free themselves entirely from the oppression of the mother country. Those who before had wavered and looked upon the signers of the Declaration as men who had rashly burned their bridges behind them now came forward and either enlisted in the army or gave of their means to its support.

Washington had been appointed by the second General Congress, Commander-in-Chief of the American forces and was on his way to Boston to assume the command. In every part of the country companies were being organized and drilled for active service against the invaders. Barent Van Houten and his company were already in the city of New York and composed part of the force encamped at Harlem Heights, where fortifications were erected for the defence of the city. Ramapo Pass was also being fortified, appropriations for the same having been made by act of the General Congress, and Fort Sidman was built near the southern mouth of the valley to protect this, the main pass through the highlands between the Hudson and the Delaware.

It was a time of energetic organization among the sons of liberty throughout the thirteen colonies, which together, formed the brightest jewel in England's crown.

Rembrandt Onderdonk, now a captain of scouts, was busily engaged in watching the movements of British war vessels on the Hudson river, and the doings of the tories and cowboys between that river and Ramapo Pass. Word had been sent him from several different points, of depredations committed by them upon the farmers of the district. Cattle and horses were stolen and the inhabitants maltreated and abused if they dared to protest against these acts of violence.

On the afternoon of the day set for the gathering of the band under Claudius Smith, there seemed to be more than the usual number of visitors at the Smith homestead in the valley. There were hardy, rough looking men arriving and departing, as though they had come to headquarters to report and receive orders ; and such in fact was the case, for Claudius was there, and the men seen going in and out were of the kind who acknowledged him as their leader and in whom they placed the utmost confidence.

He occupied a small room in the rear of what might be called the bar-room (for old man Smith kept a country tavern), and there he received his men, gave them their orders, and sent them on their way to carry out his plans.

As the shadows of night closed in around the valley the chief himself emerged from the house, and mounted his horse which had been held in readiness by a colored servant. He was well mounted on a little and beautiful black gelding, whose glistening coat denoted the care and grooming he received, and taking a bridle path down the eastern side of the valley, was soon lost to sight in the gathering twilight. Claudius continued down the valley, until he came to where the towering form of Man of War Rock could be distinguished on the western heights, when he turned sharply to the left and began to ascend the eastern range.

It was a steep and tortuous path, but the rider knew every inch of it as well as the grounds about his birthplace. He ascended until he reached the summit, when he drew rein and stood motionless as a statue. Taking a small silver whistle from his pocket, he placed it to his mouth and blew a low prolonged note. In a few seconds it was answered by a similar whistle from some rocks beyond. Again he blew a short sharp note, and then a man appeared as if rising out of the ground not five rods from where he stood. He raised his hat, gave the chief a military salute, advanced a few paces and came to a halt.

Claudius sprang from his horse, threw the bridle over his neck, and walking up to the sentinel, asked whether Cobus had arrived? "Yes," answered the man, "he is there (pointing to a ledge of rocks) with all the rest." "Take care of my horse," said the leader, and with these words he disappeared into a peculiar opening in the rocks.

The man led the horse a short distance to the north, where beneath the shelter of an immense overhanging rock he secured him to a staple fastened in the solid granite wall. This place (since known throughout that vicinity as Horse Stable Rock) would contain probably thirty or forty horses or cattle with comparative ease and comfort to the animals, and was almost perfectly secure from observation. Great hemlocks with their dense, dark foliage reaching almost to the ground, stood along the front, while beneath them grew a natural hedge of evergreen laurel with interlacing branches, which together formed an impenetrable thicket, completely hiding everything within.

The secret rendezvous of the tory band was one of the most remarkable natural caverns in existence. Situated as it was near the summit of the eastern range of the Ramapo mountains, it was well calculated for the headquarters of a gang of lawless spirits, whose doings would not stand the light of day. It also had this advantage, that during the day time no one could approach it without being discovered by the sentinel on guard, as the location commanded a view in every direction.

When Claudius entered the cavern he found nearly the whole band there. The room, which was about twenty feet square, was lighted by tallow candles set on small ledges against the side walls, and one rude chandelier hung from the center of the roof. As he entered the men rose and greeted him cordially. "I am pleased to see you all so punctual," said he, "and now, let us to business!" He took a seat at a small table in the center of the room, and thus addressed his assembled followers: "Boys," said he, "there is work to be done, there is money to be earned, and at the same time our king and country to be served. The British army will, in the near future, require provisions, for which the quartermasters will pay liberally, for they are well supplied with the yellow gold of Old England, and I see no reason why we, who are in sympathy with their cause, should not earn an honest shilling by supplying them with the beef which is now fattening in the rebel pastures around us. By doing so we will be aiding the cause of King George, and what is still more to the purpose, helping ourselves also. What have you to say to this, my men?" asked the chief, as he rose from the chair and looked around the room.

"We are ready to follow you, Captain Claud, wherever you may lead," replied his men, one and all. "And now," said Claudius, "to back up the good resolutions we have made, let us drink health to King George, the rightful sovereign of these colonies." And calling on Cobus to bring out the keg of apple brandy which had been provided for the occasion, they one and all gathered around the table, ready at their captain's word to drink to the health of his majesty.

Pewter cups holding about half a pint were produced and a liberal supply of the fiery liquid poured into each one, when Claudius gave the signal, and raising the beaker to his lips, said: "Here is long life and health to George the Third, our gracious lord and king; perdition, death, and dishonor to all his enemies!" As the last words were spoken, they drank to the sentiment, and clashing their cups together, until the mountain cavern rang again, they gave three rousing cheers for Captain Claudius Smith and the undertaking they had in hand.

"Now," said Claudius, "as you are no doubt aware, our work must be mainly done at night. And when we can capture a sufficient number of cattle or horses, it is our plan to drive them to this or some other rendezvous until we get an opportunity to run them into the British lines, where their sale will be quick and profitable." He then appointed his brother Lieutenant ; and thus was organized a band of desperadoes, which, throughout the whole revolutionary struggle was a terror to the surronnding country and made the name of tory and cowboy a stench in the nostrils of every honest man.

CHAPTER VII.

As time passed and the different results of the Revolutionary struggle transpired, now depressing to the patriotic cause, and again encouraging the actors in it to renewed effort to throw off the British yoke, events were taking place among the rural scenes where our story is laid of a character calculated to arouse the bitter vengeance of the Whigs and cause them to make a combined effort to rid themselves of the cause.

Captain Onderdonk, as before stated, had been informed of the depredations committed in various quarters by the tories and cowboys under the command of the bandit chief Claudius, but had been kept from attempting their punishment by his other duties along the Hudson River, and in the eastern part of the district, until now, it had become a necessity to make a grand effort to rid the country of this pest, or give over a fair portion of the Province to their control. As to the latter alternative, Captain Rem. was not constituted that way, and determined to teach them a lesson that should not be forgotten during the remainder of the struggle.

At this time he was engaged with the greater part of his company in patrolling the west bank of the Hudson from Verdrietige Hook to King's Ferry. The American army had met with disaster at White Plains, and had retreated and crossed the river at the latter place, while detachments of the royalist forces were occupying the east bank and the country beyond for a considerable distance. Under these conditions Rem. did not deem it prudent to leave the river at that point entirely unprotected and without a man to watch the movements of the vessels of war which were continually moving either up or down the stream and annoying the inhabitants who resided along its banks.

He therefore selected twenty of the most reliable men of his company and set out immediately for the vicinity of Ramapo Pass. The remainder he left in charge of his brother Dirck (who acted as his Lieutenant) to keep watch of the movements of the enemy there. Rem. knew from the report which Black George had made some time before pretty nearly where he might expect to find the rendezvous of Claudius and his band, but to make it certain not to miss the place he determined to get George to act as guide.

Captain Onderdonk and his little company arrived at the Onderdonk homestead just as the sun began to paint the eastern horizon with the glorious colors of a summer morning, having marched all that night. The household had not yet begun the labors of the day—in fact some of them were still enjoying their morning nap—but Black George was found at the barn attending to the stock and overseeing several young darkies who were engaged in doing the morning chores.

Captain Rem. was received by his family with expressions of joy ; and Katharine rushed into his arms, and hung about his neck with all the effusive tenderness of a loving sister for a favorite brother. Some time had passed since he had visited the old homestead, and he was therefore received by the whole household with more than the usual demonstrations of gladness. The staunch old Whig, his father, immediately ordered a substantial breakfast to be prepared for the whole company, and the services of every servant and member of the family were called into requisition for the occasion.

Black George, the chief of the retainers in the employ of old Martinus, was especially busy to make the visit of "Mars Rem." and his company as pleasant as possible. Rem. was led into the great living room of the mansion by his sister and for more than an hour was engaged in answering questions in regard to his own doings, how the cause was progressing in the different localities he had visited in the line of duty, how his brother Dirck fared, and the thousand and one questions suggested by parental love and interest in the cause of liberty.

Breakfast being ready the company was ordered to stack arms and then was conducted into the great kitchen, where the table was found loaded with everything calculated to tempt the appetite. Having been on the march since the evening previous, the men were in condition to do justice to the viands set before them. After breakfast Rem. told his men to take a good rest, as in all probability the coming night would be one of exertion, for he determined if possible to find the rendezvous of the cowboys and drive them from the vicinity.

In the afternoon Rem. consulted with George and they mapped out a plan of procedure to be carried out the coming night.

The sun had scarcely vanished behind the western hills when Captain Rem. called his men to arms, and headed by Black George they began their march in search of the cowboy band. Striking across the meadow land to the north of the farm house, they soon entered the forest which extended to the foot of the mountain range, and after an hour's tramp came to the base of the mountains.

The location of the cavern had been so minutely described by George that Captain Rem. thought he could find it without assistance. He therefore divided his command into two detachments of ten each. George was placed at the head of one of them as guide, while Rem. led the other; the plan of attack being to approach the stronghold of the cowboys from two sides at once and thus close in around the place and prevent all escape.

Slowly and silently they ascended the mountain. Not a twig snapped, not a footfall was heard as they, with difficulty, clambered over the precipitous rocks, or crawled through the thick underbrush which covered the eastern side of the range. At last the two parties reached the summit and deployed into skirmish lines. They then advanced toward each other expecting to take the bandits by surprise. They approached to within a hundred yards of where they felt certain the cavern was situated when out upon the night air came the report of a dozen rifles, resounding through the mountain valleys and among the hills like the crack of doom. Several of the attacking party went down at the first fire, and at least one of them was mortally wounded.

Captain Rem. tried to rally his men, and indeed they returned the fire as best they could; but they were fighting an invisible foe who had been prepared for their coming, and were hiding behind every tree and rock, and with perfect safety picked off their enemies as they caught sight of them moving among the trees upon the summit of the ridge.

There was only one remedy, and that was to retreat and get out of the scrape as best they could. Rem. therefore gave the order, and down the mountain side they went, carrying their wounded with them. That there had been a traitor in camp was certain, and the only way in which it could be explained was that some person whose sympathies were with the tory band had discovered their object while resting at the Onderdonk homestead, or had divined their purpose when seen on their march from the Hudson.

To say that Captain Onderdonk was disappointed at the outcome of the expedition did not do justice to his feelings on the subject; but like the true soldier that he was, he was not totally disheartened, and consoled himself and followers with the promise that they should do better next time, and he further determined that that next time should not be far distant in the future. The next day he returned with his company to their camp near the Hudson.

CHAPTER VIII.

Barent Van Houten had been with his company through the disastrous battles of Long Island and White Plains and in the retreat through New Jersey, and was now stationed with it as part of the force occupying the fortifications at Ramapo Pass. This brought him within a short distance of home, and of the one who next to his country held the most sacred place in his affections. He therefore took advantage of the opportunity, and procuring a furlough for a few days, rode over to the old neighborhood. He found all the friends there in good health and spirits and overjoyed to receive him safe and sound after his long absence.

For Mary Demaray the months since he left her to proceed with his company to the seat or war had passed on leaden wings. She was aware of the dangers which surrounded him, of the bloody battles he had participated in and of the defeats the army had sustained of which himself and company formed a part, and consequently she had been ill at ease under the circumstances. But her faith in the cause had been strong, and when she heard the good old dominie pray every Sabbath for the success of the American arms, she had a firm reliance that the God of battles would in the end favor the cause of the Colonies.

After Barent had given a detailed account to his parents of all the incidents and accidents he had experienced during the time he had been with the army, of all the sufferings and sacrifices endured by the patriots composing the army and all the other information he was possessed of, he rode over to the dwelling of old Bernhard Demaray. He was received there by the whole family with every demonstration of joy at his safe return from the campaigns in which he had been an actor, and for an hour was kept busy relating to the old gentleman all the incidents of the war coming under his immediate notice. To Mary, his betrothed, he poured out the aspirations of his heart as together they talked over their prospects for the future and laid the plans which they expected to see realized when this unnatural struggle should come to an end.

As the reader already knows, Barent was commissioned a Lieutenant when the war began, but he had since been promoted to a captaincy for brave and meritorious conduct on the field of battle. Of course Mary felt a certain pride in the promotion of her gallant lover, who had, in the most unselfish manner, thrown his whole soul into the cause of his country, not knowing which way the scale might turn, and recking not of the consequences, if in the end the balance should turn against him. She recognized his noble nature, and was proud of the valor he had displayed in many a bloody battle with the enemies of liberty, and gave him all the love her warm heart was capable of, and which was reciprocated by Barent, to whom she was more than all the earth beside.

But this dalliance with his lady love could not continue, for his furlough was about expiring and he must be off to duty. So taking an affectionate leave of Mary, and bidding farewell to his family and friends, he returned to his post at Fort Sidman among the Ramapo mountains.

About this time, the autumn of 1776, the spirit

of the Americans was at a low ebb. The army had been chased across New Jersey and into Pennsylvania, by Cornwallis, and was quartered along the banks of the Delaware. But an encouraging event took place, when Washington, on the 26th December, recrossed the river and won the battle of Trenton. This raised the hopes of the people, so that enlistments became more frequent and supplies more plentiful.

In that battle the Americans captured one thousand Hessians, slew their leader and escaped back across the Delaware with the loss of two killed in the action and two others frozen to death. A few days after this, viz., January 3rd, 1777, having again recrossed the Delaware, Washington fell upon a detachment lying at Princeton, routed them, took three hundred prisoners, and by a rapid march reached the heights of Morristown in safety. This last event set the country wild with joy and raised the hopes of the friends of liberty to a greater pitch than ever before.

While these great events were transpiring in New Jersey, matters of smaller calibre, but not less interesting to those engaged, were taking place among the hills of Ramapo. Claudius, after the repulse of the expedition sent against him under the command of Captain Onderdonk, became more audacious in his manner and actions, and boldly led his men into the open country and seized the horses and cattle belonging to the farmers of the vicinity ; and if any resistance was offered, did not hesitate to kill in order to accomplish his designs. These depredations were becoming of such common occurrence and the inhabitants were so thoroughly terrorized, that in the fall of 1778 complaint was made to the Commander-in-Chief, whose headquarters were then at the Suffern mansion at the southern end of Ramapo valley.

The work of dislodging this band of marauders, as time passed, became difficult. Their emissaries were scattered over all that part of the country which now comprises the counties of Orange and Rockland in New York, and Bergen and Passaic in New Jersey. Every move was watched and every action of the patriots was noted by these traitors to human liberty, and reported to the cowboy chief. As may be seen, therefore, it was an undertaking of considerable magnitude to rid the neighborhood of this well organized band of villains.

Through the center of this district which they infested, ran the range of mountains known as the Kakiatt, or Ramapo range, in the fastnesses of which were located their hiding places. The complaints against the bandits were so many and became so urgent, that Washington finally, after counseling with officers who knew the difficulties and dangers attending the business, selected Captain Rembrandt Onderdonk, with his company of scouts, to pursue this band of outlaws, until they were all either killed, captured, or driven out of the country.

With this end in view, the General sent for Rem., who at the time was with his company near King's Ferry on the Hudson. Rem. soon appeared at headquarters ready for business. He was conducted into the presence of Washington by Captain Barent Van Houten, who had lately been appointed one of his aids.

"Captain Onderdonk," said Washington, "I have sent for you to confer upon business of a very important nature. It appears from many reports received at these headquarters that the mountain range between this point and King's Ferry is infested by a well organized band of tories and cowboys, led by a most unscrupulous and cunning man by the name of Claudius Smith. You have been recommended by those in whom I place the utmost confidence as the one person above all others to command the expedition I intend to send against them. I will not force this command upon you. I know the danger and difficulties attending an undertaking of this kind. In fact I will accept none but volunteers, both officers and men. What say you Captain Onderdonk, can we have your services."

"General," answered Rem., "I have enlisted for the war and expect to serve until victory crowns our efforts or my life shall last, and am at the service of my country in any capacity the Commander-in-Chief may see fit to designate."
"Thank you, Captain Onderdonk ! I am pleased to find you willing to undertake this business and believe you will be able to accomplish what you are about to set out to do," said the general. "Captain Van Houten will accompany you, and

when the soldiers of this post are drawn up for inspection, you have my permission to call for as many volunteers as you need to reinforce your own command, and for the success of the expedition you have my best wishes."

So saying Washington dismissed Captain Rem., who immediately proceeded with Barent to recruit his ranks.

When the men comprising the garrison of Fort Sidman were ordered out for inspection, Barent announced the wishes of the General. Captain Rem. selected twenty-five men out of hundreds who volunteered their service, and leaving them at the fort until he could bring his old company from King's Ferry, he bade Barent good bye and started on his return to camp.

CHAPTER IX.

At the base of the mountains where Call Hollow pierces the range toward the north, was situated at the time of which we write a somewhat dilapidated log house. Its surroundings were wild and forbidding. The dark green foliage of the old hemlocks which grew around it almost hid the structure from observation, and made the place look dismal and gloomy in the extreme. The sole occupant of this cheerless abode was an old woman of probably seventy-five. Though stooping somewhat under the weight of years, Aunt Hester, as she was called by all who knew her, was still active and quick in her movements, and her black, piercing eyes retained the brightness of youth.

Throughout the whole neighborhood she was known as a fortune teller, and by the superstitious portion of the inhabitants she was suspected of holding secret communications with the gentleman in black. Strange stories of uncanny doings in the old house were told by the people who had occasion to pass the place at night. Curious illuminations of the house had been seen in the small hours of the morning, when the old lady had guests of strange character, and goings on were heard and seen which had the appearance of ghostly revels. In fact the old woman had been seen by several (whose words were hard to doubt) dancing with her naked feet in the midst of glowing coals, while some one who had the appearance of Satan himself was playing upon a fiddle to make the music for her.

Of course, all these stories caused the timid ones to shun the place, and therefore Aunt Hester was not troubled or overburdened with visitors. It was only now and then, some rustic Romeo ventured there to consult her in regard to his future, or to find out how his suit would be received by his intended Juliet. It was seldom any one would own to having thus consulted her, but still it was surmised that others, whose pretentions to greater intelligence was well known, had crossed the old dame's palm with the gold so necessary to future insight, and received from her the horoscope of their nativity.

Be this as it may, one thing is certain, that on a dark and stormy night in the early part of the winter of 1778, when the north wind came howling down Call Hollow and the old hemlocks bent and swirled under the wintry blast, a stalwart form might have been seen knocking for admission at the door of the old log house. As the man stood there waiting to be admitted, the snow, driven by the fitful gusts of wind, whirled around him and dashed into his face with terrible force. He became impatient and knocked long and loudly. At last the door opened slowly and the old woman asked who was there and what was wanted. "In the first place I want to get in out of this infernal storm," said the man, as he pushed through the half open door, "and in the next place I have come to find out what is to befall me in the future?" "Why should you come to me on such an errand, Claudius Smith? Can't you let an old woman like me rest in peace," replied the old dame. "Well, Aunt Hester," said Claudius, (for it was he) "it is said in all the country round that you can tell what the future holds in store for us poor mortals, and so I have come to you for that purpose. See, here is the glittering gold which is the open sesame to your black art!" saying which, he laid an English sovereign in her hand.

"Claudius Smith," said Aunt Hester, her small black eyes glittering in the light of the tallow candle, like those of a basilisk, "you don't want *me* to tell you of the future. You know what that will be without my telling; therefore go, leave me in peace, and trouble no more a decrepit old woman!" She knew of the doings of the man who now stood before her; of how unscrupulous he was, and how merciless toward those who offended him in any way. She therefore tried to put him off in the manner stated above.

But the tory chief would not be denied, and insisted that she should read the future for him. "Well," said she, "if you will have it, and nothing else will do, why so be it," and suiting the action to the words, she brought out a small pine table and placed it in the centre of the room. Upon this table she placed a pack of common playing cards and a glass half filled with water.

"Sit there," said she to Claudius, as she set a chair at one side of the table. She stood at the opposite side and taking up the pack of cards began to shuffle them in a peculiar way and finally spread some of them upon the table, while she kept the remainder in her hands. "Now draw out three cards," said she, at the same time extending to him the part of the pack she had retained.

Claudius did as he was told and drew out three cards. "What have you got," asked the dame. The tory leader spread the three cards face up upon the table. "I have the six, four and trey of spades," replied he. "Thirteen!" groaned the old woman. "Woe! woe! to you man!"

"Now what have we here?" said she, as she raised the half filled glass of water and looked into it. "I see a beautiful maiden, with sparkling blue eyes and with golden curls. She is sitting in a rustic arbor overgrown with creeping vines. A young man approaches and she receives him with joy! Now she is gone! Again I see her, but frowns are in the place of smiles and anger has taken the place of joy! The vision disappears, and another takes its place!" she said, as with trembling hand and tragic manner she raised the glass still higher and gazed as if entranced into its limpid depths.

"I see a burning building. The flames are shooting skyward. Armed men are around it, and the family whose home it was, are vainly trying to save their household goods. The armed band is gathering the horses and cattle, and now at the command of one who seems to be their leader, they march away, taking the farmer's horses and cattle with them. But another and a stranger apparition appears! I see the same armed band, led by the same leader, in deadly combat with a larger force. Blood is flowing freely and dead men lie around. At last the band is overpowered and all are taken prisoners that remain alive except the leader and three others, who escape by flight. Once more! the fates are propitious and another scene passes before my eyes! A country village with court house and jail and now a gallows comes into view! Upon the scaffold under it stand four men, one of whom is the leader of the armed band!

Officers of the law are in attendance, and soldiers of the patriot army surround the gallows! Lo! the rope is cut, and all four are launched into eternity! Thus have I told your future, Claudius Smith! You would have it so, and I am not to blame!"

"You lie, you weather beaten hag!" shouted Claudius. "That is not my horoscope! You are trying to play upon my fears and only that you are a woman I should tear your old heart from your shrunken body!"

"I have told you the truth," said old Hester, "and now you may do your worst. I do not fear you! You may kill an old and unprotected woman, but what would it benefit you? You would add one more sin to the many for which your guilty soul must answer. And that is all!"

The words of Claudius had aroused the old woman's ire, and though the heavens should fall, she would not take back a word, nor change in the slightest degree, the horrible horoscope she had read him.

Claudius, though disappointed and angered at the outcome of his visit to the old hag at Call

Hollow, set out on his return to the headquarters of his band. On his way through the mountains he had ample time to think over the occurrences of the evening, and though he made more than one resolution to throw the whole thing off his mind, his thoughts would constantly revert to the old woman's dire prophecy. In common with many people of the period there was in his composition an element of superstition which caused him, in many instances, to do things totally at variance (as his friends and comrades thought) with his usual good judgment. After a toilsome journey among rocks, through underbrush, and over fallen tree tops, he arrived at the cave and threw himself upon a couch for a good rest.

CHAPTER X.

The year 1777 was one of great military activity in the Colonies, or, as had been proclaimed by the Declaration, the United States. The struggle for independence might be said to have reached its climax at the end of that year. Princeton, Bennington and Brandywine had been fought, and the situation even then was favorable to the American arms. But when, on the night of the 17th of October, the signal fires were lighted announcing the capture of Burgoyne, the whole country was elevated to the highest pitch of joy. From Lake Champlain to the Gulf of Mexico there was feasting and rejoicing. The fine army under the veteran General Burgoyne, in its march from Canada to form a junction with Clinton at New York, never anticipated so serious a check, and its officers never expected that the ragamuffin army under Gates would even be a hindrance to their victorious march.

But the fortunes of war are always uncertain, and Bemis' Heights, Saratoga and Stillwater taught them a lesson they did not soon forget. In South Carolina and Georgia, also, the half starved and squalid troops of Marion and Sumter, which had been hiding in swamps and forests, now came forth, and with renewed energy, attacked the British garrisons and harrassed them by unexpected forays, until they were compelled to leave their outposts in the interior and retire to the coast.

Thus the prospects which before these events were gloomy and depressing, became brighter and more cheering for the patriot cause.

It was the latter part of this same year and shortly after his appearance at the old log house, that Claudius made a secret visit to the Onderdonk homestead. He knew that Rem. had been commissioned to hunt him down and to extirpate his band if possible, but still he determined to find out from Katharine herself the state of her feelings toward him. The tory chief loved her with all the fervor of which his selfish heart was capable, and believed that Katharine in a measure reciprocated those feelings.

He therefore, very unexpectedly to the whole family, appeared at the mansion, and soon learned from her, that under no circumstances would she, the sister of Captain Rem. Onderdonk, and the daughter of a staunch old Whig, become the bride of an enemy to her country and the cause so dear to her heart. Claudius knew well the stock from which she sprung and knew just as well the uselessness of trying to alter her mind by pleadings, no matter how eloquent they might be. He therefore took leave of her with courteous words and polite manner, but with dire hate at heart and half formed resolutions of vengeance in his mind.

Captain Rem. and his company, though they had been scouring the mountains and hunting through every gorge and valley in the range and had even thoroughly explored the cavern that was formerly the rendezvous of the tory gang had been unsuccessful thus far in accomplishing their purpose. The emissaries of Claudius had kept him well posted in regard to their movements and he had scattered his band and kept them under cover for the present only to be gathered again when the time was more propitious.

THE COWBOY OF RAMAPO VALLEY. 73

One day in the early spring of 1778, Black George came running almost breathless from the direction of the forest north of the Onderdonk dwelling, and calling the old gentleman aside, said: "Mas' Onderdonk, de cowboys am comin' sure! I seed dem from whar I wus cuttin' wood jist beyant de swamp! Dar am more den forty ob dem, and I am mos' sartin dat young Claudius Smit am de boss ob de gang! Dey aint comin' fer no good, and I better git de boys togedder fer to be ready fer em, eh, Mas' Onderdonk?" "Yes, George," replied the old man, "but if there are as many of them as you think, we will hardly be able to withstand them." "We kin do de bes' we kin, Mas' Onderdonk," returned George. And having received permission, he called the work hands of the farm, white and black together, to defend the place as best they could. The whole of them when assembled numbered ten, young and old.

They were armed with anything that came handy—axes, pitchforks and iron bars being among the weapons provided, George and old Martinus only, being armed with rifles. "Now," said George (when he had assumed the command), "we better meet em at de barn, fer dey'll git dar fust. I'll take Sam and de boys to help me dar, and you, Mas' Onderdonk, and Cæsar kin stay at de house and take kar ob old missus and Miss Katharine."

After making this disposition of his garrison, George constituted himself a picket to watch the movements of the marauders. He placed himself behind one of the small outbuildings north of the barn where he could note the first appearance of the enemy from the direction they were expected to come. It was now nearly dark and he had not been on guard more than half an hour, when through the gathering gloom he saw some moving objects at the edge of the forest. He called Sam's attention to them and while they were trying to ascertain what it meant, they were astonished at the appearance of probably thirty well armed men, approaching from a direction at nearly right angles from where the moving objects were first seen.

Black George, rifle in hand, stepped out from the covering building and called out: "Hi dar! halt! what you want har? Stop, right whar you is! You har me? Don't you come any ferder, or I'll let you know what am inside dis fowlin' piece!" But they paid no attention to his command and came on secure in overwhelming numbers. "Take dat, den! dod bust yer bad skins!" shouted George, as he raised his rifle and fired into the crowd. There was a yell of pain from some one in the gang; but on they came, and before the little band of defenders could make any resistance they were overpowered and taken prisoners.

After disposing of the men and boys at the barn, Claudius, (who was in command,) gave orders to collect the horses and cattle, while himself and a couple of his men went to the mansion. Old Martinus, who saw the folly of attempting to make a stand against such a large force, was found sitting on the porch. Katharine and her mother were inside of the house, and though badly frightened, were attending to their household duties. As Claudius approached the old man, he bade him good evening, and in his most suave tones asked after his health. He said he was very sorry to inconvenience him, but that the King's forces were in need of provisions of all kinds and he was therefore under the necessity of confiscating his cattle and horses. "The soldiers of the King must be supplied," said he, "and his enemies should be compelled to bear their share of the burden!"

"Claudius," said the old man, "I know what you came for. I also know that you have the power to take what you wish; therefore make no excuses, but admit honestly that you came to rob and plunder us, not that you may supply the British army, but that you mean to drive off my cattle and horses and sell them for your own benefit."

"Well," said Claudius, "let it be as you say; I will not argue with you, for argument is generally unprofitable and takes up precious time." Just then Katharine appeared in the doorway and was greeted by the tory chief with a courteous salutation. "Good evening, Katharine! I am happy to meet you!" said he. "Shame upon you Claudius! for what you are doing," said she, and turning to her father remarked: "We are being stung by the viper we have warmed, but we will let him know that, though they may rob us of our possessions, they can never crush the spirit of the true sons and daughters of liberty. You may do your worst, I only despise you!" "I am sorry you have so bad an opinion of the soldiers of the King, but necessity must be our plea," answered Claudius.

Turning to his men who had gathered in front of the house with the cattle and horses belonging to the Onderdonk farm, ready to be driven away, he said : " Drive on, boys ; we have a long way to go ; and seeing the night is going to be very dark, two of you go back and fire the barns that we may have some light by the way." In a few moments a bright blaze shot heavenward and lit up the surrounding landscape. With a low and courteous bow to Katharine, he mounted his horse and with the rest of his band disappeared in the darkness.

"What have they done with George, and the rest of the boys?" asked Katharine, as the flames burst out anew from the great Dutch barn. "I will go and find out," replied the old gentleman ; and calling Cæsar they went to the barn and found that George and his companions had been securely locked in the granary, where they would certainly have perished but for the timely coming of their liberators.

"Oh dear!" groaned George as he came out and viewed the burning buildings. "You rascal tories! you'll hab ter pay fer dis night's work! Jis wait till Mas' Rem. comes back and den I guess dar'll be an overhaulin' of dis bizness! Oh! Mas' Onderdonk! dey haint lef' a horse nor a cow on de hull place. Dem tory debils done took 'em all sure! Sarten as my name am George, I'll help put up de job to make 'em pay for dis night's doins!" And with many such threats of vengeance, the poor negro sat down upon a rock in the barn yard and wept like a child at the destruction accomplished by the outlaws.

The horses and cattle were driven and sold to a detachment of the British army lying at a point about three miles north of Tappan, in the valley of the Hackensack. Their plan of dispersing and seeking their rendezvous separately, after disposing of their booty, made it almost impossible to punish these marauders or to intercept them while on one of their forays after cattle, as their depredations were nearly always committed in the night.

CHAPTER XI.

The winter of 1778 was really the most gloomy period of the war. Washington, with the main body of the American army was encamped at Valley Forge, in the northeastern part of Pennsylvania. The clothing of the men was worn out and they came upon the parade ground with rags dangling from their persons. The shoes of many of them were gone, and the tracks made by their bloody feet could be seen on the frozen ground of this valley of despair. The continental paper money had become so much depreciated that even an officer's pay would scarcely keep him in clothing. The winter was one of the coldest ever experienced in that latitude, and the condition of the army on that account was worse than can be described. To add to the miseries of destitution and nakedness, sickness became prevalent, and no medicines were to be had.

But through all these adversities the fires of patriotism still burned brightly and the spirit of devotion to the cause of liberty animated their hearts and upheld them in the determination to shake off the British yoke. The picture of the great hero on his knees, amid these scenes of suffering and wretchedness, praying to the God of battles for the deliverance of his beloved country from the yoke of the oppressor, was a sure precursor of the end.

On the 6th day of February, France, through the influence of Benjamin Franklin, acknowledged the independence of the United States, and agreed to send a fleet to their assistance. Thus things began to look brighter as spring opened, and when, on the 28th of the following June, the battle of Monmouth was fought and won by the American forces, the country again became hopeful.

Captain Barent Van Houten, though acting as one of Washington's aids while his headquarters was at the Suffern mansion, near Fort Sidman, had remained with his company when the Commander-in-Chief went south to Valley Forge. The time had passed slowly and without much to interest them, as their only duty was to guard the pass, until the summer of 1779, when his company, among others, was detached to make part of the force of General Wayne to attack Stony Point.

It was a warm morning in early July that the order came to "fall in," and in a short time the detachment was making its way along the old King's road, leading from the point of the mountain to King's Ferry. It was a hot and dusty march and quite a number of the men succumbed to the overpowering heat.

At a point some five or six miles south of their destination they found Captain Rem. Onderdonk and his company of scouts awaiting them. He had received orders to form a junction with the men from Fort Sidman, and, together, they took up the march toward the fort on the Hudson.

Some time had elapsed since Barent and Rem. had met, and many things had transpired in the old neighborhood which interested them both. As they journeyed together toward what might be their final destination, Rem. told of the destruction of the barns on the old farm, how the cowboys under Claudius had run off the cattle and horses belonging to his father and how he would make them feel his vengeance if he was spared long enough to accomplish it. "Barent," said Rem., "I shall not rest until that infernal band of thieves and bandits are destroyed, and if I come safely through the coming fight, I shall attend strictly to that business until it is finished. My company was reinforced for that purpose and I scoured the mountain range from end to end to find them, but thus far they have eluded me. Their spies are located in every neighborhood and in every hamlet throughout the district; but if I once strike their trail I will not leave it until I have run them to earth."

"I hope you may be successful," returned Barent, "but you have a cunning fox to deal with, and I fear he will give you a long chase before he is caught." "Well," said Rem., "I shall not leave a stone unturned to destroy them and rid the land of their presence, for there is no safety for either age or sex so long as these scoundrels are in existence."

At the distance of about a mile from Stony Point the detachment was halted, and, through the growing darkness, they saw approaching another body of men. It was the battalion which had landed at Sandy Beach on the Hudson, and the two detachments meeting there were to form the attacking force under General Wayne. It was now nearly dark, and while the men stood at rest in the ranks, the general rode down the line and thus addressed them :

"I expect every man to do his duty ! That fort must be taken, and not a musket must be fired ! Let every man draw the charge from his piece and be sure to fix his bayonet securely, for it is only with cold steel we must capture it !"

Captain Rem. Onderdonk was selected to lead the forlorn hope which was to attack the fort on the west side as a feint, while the main body should make the attempt from the east, or river side.

As is well known, a negro who knew the path, led the main body through the marsh between the river and the bluff upon which the fort was located. As the men still stood in the ranks Captain Rem. stepped in front of them to call for volunteers to form the forlorn hope. "I want," said he, "only such men as fear God and not man !

Let those who are willing to volunteer step one pace to the front!" As one man, the whole detachment advanced a step. Rem. then selected fifty men, and under cover of the darkness immediately started for the fort.

The main body followed until it came to the foot of the promontory upon which the fort was built. When they arrived there they halted and remained there awaiting the attack of the forlorn hope. All at once the rattle of musketry was heard on the western slope and the shouts of the men as they made the attack!

While this was going on and while the forlorn hope was being mowed down like wheat before the sickle, the main body under the immediate command of Mad Anthony, was led by the old negro through the morass and up the narrow path leading to the fort.

They had nearly gained the summit, when they were discovered by the garrison and a devastating fire was poured into them. Almost at the first fire General Wayne was wounded in the head. "Carry me at the head of the column," said the general. His order was obeyed, and upon a stretcher he led the impetuous charge of his men, who with fixed bayonets carried everything before them.

It was the work of only a few minutes to capture the fort, so overpowering was the rush of the Americans. But the forlorn hope suffered fearfully. Of the fifty men composing it only ten survived; but among these was the heroic leader. The British loss was six hundred in killed, wounded and prisoners, while the American loss was only one hundred.

Captain Rem., whose attack and feint upon the western side of the fort had contributed so much to its capture, was complimented by General Wayne for his bravery and good conduct in leading the forlorn hope. A large quantity of amunition and military stores, of which the American army stood in great need, were taken.

The fort was taken July 15th, and the next day about half of the prisoners, under the escort of Captains Rem. and Barent with their two companies, took the road back to Fort Sidman. They had got about one-half the distance between the two points when night overtook them, and they determined to halt until daylight. Their whole force consisted of only about seventy-five men, while their prisoners numbered more than three hundred. They therefore took possession of the barn and outbuildings belonging to the old country tavern just west of Coe's corner on the old King's road, and for safety locked the prisoners in them. After placing a strong guard around the buildings the officers took lodgings in the tavern for the night.

About 2 o'clock the next morning a great commotion was heard by the sentinels on guard, among the prisoners confined in the barn, and believing that they were about to rise and overpower them, they fired into the barn. This firing in the still hours of the early morning, immediately aroused the officers and soldiers not on duty, who rushed to the barn to find that four of the prisoners had been killed and a number wounded.

The cause of the commotion inside was found to have been a quarrel ending in a knock down fight among the captured soldiers. In the morning the dead men were buried behind the barn, where their remains still lie; but their ghosts often (so the inhabitants say) stalk abroad and to this day haunt a house which in after years was built upon the site of the old barn. After the burial of the dead prisoners, they resumed their march and toward night of the same day arrived at Fort Sidman.

CHAPTER XII.

While the events described in the previous chapter were passing in different parts of the land, a terrible and mysterious occurrence took place in the Onderdonk family. The morning after the capture of Stony Point the old man and most of the family were about attending to the morning's work and preparing to rebuild the barns which had been destroyed by the tories, when the old lady appeared, and with blanched face and trembling voice, asked whether any one had seen Katharine. They all returned a negative answer. She had not been seen by any of the family since the previous night, when she had bidden her parents good night and retired to her room.

A search was immediately instituted about the premises, and every member of the family began an investigation to find the cause of her disappearance. No noises had been heard and there were no signs of a struggle in her room, as every article of furniture therein was in its place. Her couch was undisturbed, showing that it had not been occupied by her during the night. Every piece of woodland, every thicket, and, in fact, every place throughout the neighborhood was searched by the family and friends ; but at nightfall they all returned to the house unsuccessful. She had disappeared completely and myteriously and no one could account for it.

Of course there were suspicions—but there was really no foundation for them until Black George the next morning reported that he had found the marks of footsteps in the earth under the window of Katharine's room. He insisted that they were the tracks of two large men, as they were of immense size. He immediately set out to follow the trail and only lost it some distance in the forest north of the dwelling. The direction taken by the men whose footsteps had been discovered, caused Katharine's friends to suspect that Claudius Smith had something to do with her unaccountable disappearance.

It was well known among them that the tory

chief had been a suitor for her hand and that she had rejected his offer with disdain; but they did not think it possible for him to commit a crime of this kind. They knew his crafty and covetous nature, and that he would not hesitate to commit almost any kind of depredation if he saw in it any financial gain for himself; but they did not dream that Claudius would take so much trouble for either love or vengeance's sake.

As might be supposed, her family, and especially her father and mother, were overcome and nearly crazed by the occurrence, and Black George, who loved the young misuss, and looked up to her almost as to a superior being, was literally crushed in spirit by the sad incident. He was sent to Fort Sidman to inform Rem. of his sister's strange disappearance, and arrived there just as Rem. and Barent with their companies had returned from Stony Point.

"Oh! Mas' Rem., dis am awful! My goodness! how kin I tell you! Oh! it am terrible!" cried George, as he attempted to inform Rem. of what had happened. "What ails you, George? What causes you to act in this manner," said

Rem. "Come, tell me what brings you here? How are the folks at home?" asked he. "De folks am all well what am home; but Miss Katharine ain't home and we don't know whar she am gone," answered George. And then he told the story to Rem. as best he could, between groans and threats of vengeance against her abductors.

"Can it be possible," said Rem., turning to Barent, who had heard part of George's story, "that she has been abducted by that infernal tory? I know she disdainfully and in cutting words refused an offer of his hand, but I can scarcely believe that Claudius, merely to gratify his spite, would commit a crime so detestable and add another incentive to hunt him down like a dog."

"This is terrible!" said Barent, "and if there is anything I can do to aid you in this emergency I wish you would command me." "I do not know in what manner you can assist me except that your better acquaintance with Colonel Malcolm, the commander of this post, might help me to procure a furlough for a few days," answered

Rem. "Come," said Barent, "we will go to him at once." And together they proceeded to the headquarters of the commander. Colonel Malcolm forthwith granted the request and George and Rem. immediately set out on their journey home.

On their way to the Onderdonk dwelling, George gave Rem. all the particulars in regard to the disappearance of his sister that he was possessed of. "Dey mus' be slashin' big fellers dat owned dem tracks, fer you know, Mas' Rem., dat my feet ain't much like a baby's, and I do declar, dat bofe of mine could git into one ob dem tracks," said George, as they journeyed along.

In due time they arrived at the house where Rem. found his father and mother, bent under the weight of sorrow that had overwhelmed them and the whole household in a state of consternation. He consoled the old people as well as he could by telling them that he thought no harm would come to Katharine, and that in all probability she would be found and returned to them in safety.

He examined the ground around the house and with the help of George followed the trail made by the abductors far into the forest and made one discovery which George had failed to notice. That was the place where two horses had been standing, as shown by the ground being stamped over by their feet. Here, no doubt, was the place where Katherine had been placed upon one of the horses and taken to some secure point in the mountains, but where that was, no one thus far could tell.

After finding out all he could and encouraging the old farmer and his wife to the best of his ability, Rem. was obliged to leave the old home and repair to the scene of duty. He had intended ere this to have started on another hunt for the cowboy band, but other duties had kept him from it, and the state of affairs was still such as to prevent his immediate prosecution of that purpose.

CHAPTER XIII.

The latter part of the year 1779 had been a period of gloom and misfortune to the American arms, especially in the South, where, at Savannah, the combined American and French forces had been repulsed by the British army occupying that city.

Affairs at the North were also in such a condition as to keep our hero and his friend Barent fully employed at Fort Sidman and King's Ferry, and the west bank of the Hudson which it was necessary to patrol constantly. At this time, the beginning of the year 1780, quite a large detachment of the American army was stationed at Tappan, where Washington occupied the DeWint mansion as his headquarters. The old building still stands, as strong and substantial as ever. It is built of stone excepting the front, which is composed of brick brought from Holland, and the date, 1700, is masoned into the front, where it is still as legible as when placed there, one hundred and ninety-four years ago.

Sir Henry Clinton, the British commander at New York, was continually sending out bands of tories and regulars to devastate the country within a radius of thirty miles of the city. One of these bands marched up the Hackensack Valley, burning the farm houses and, in many instances, murdering old and decrepit men whose extreme age incapacitated them for military duty. This predatory gang burned the settlement of Closter in New Jersey, and bayoneted in cold blood several Whigs who were too old to run away or make any resistance.

About this time, too, there was enacted a tragedy which should have caused the blush of shame to mantle the cheek of every actor in it. Colonel Baylor, with part of a troop of light horse, had taken possession of a barn for the night in a neighborhood called old Tappan, about a mile west of Tappan proper. While sleeping, they were surprised and surrounded by a large detachment of British and tories, under the command of a blood-thirsty officer of the British army. They were so thoroughly taken by surprise that they did not have the opportunity to fire a shot, and surrendered at discretion. Instead of being held as prisoners of war the most of them were immediately shot or bayoneted. Every one of them would have been butchered but for the humanity of a British officer who dared to disobey the orders of his commander. Their bodies were thrown into the vats of an old tannery near by.

Such actions had the effect of putting a more malignant face on a struggle which already had begun to assume all the horrors of civil strife; and it aroused the patriots to more determined efforts and gave them reason for retaliation when the occasion offered.

The duties of the revolutionary scouts were onerous in the extreme. They were expected to patrol thoroughly certain portions of the country, intercept and repulse, if possible, these predatory bands, and report to the headquarters of the commander of the district, any movements of the larger bodies of the enemy. They were in fact the police of the time, protecting the non-combatants and circumventing the evil disposed persons who always, in time of war, take advantage of the condition of the country to prey upon their neighbors.

Thus we may understand that Captain Rem. and his company had enough to engage their attention and to fully employ their time.

On the evening Miss Katharine Onderdonk disappeared she had retired to her room about eleven o'clock. The air was somewhat sultry and hot, and sitting down at the bedside she took up a book that was lying upon the table and began to read. She had been reading perhaps half an hour and was just upon the point of retiring when a strong hand grasped her from behind and a heavy blanket was thrown over her head, completely smothering any outcry that she might attempt to make. She was then lifted bodily from the chair and, the window being raised by some one from the outside, was placed gently upon her feet on the ground. The two men then picked her up and carried her, with the blanket still about her, until they arrived at the edge of the forest about half a mile from the house. They then lifted the blanket from her, and placed a heavy bandage over her eyes. "Come," said one of the men, "it is easier for us that you should walk, and it will be more pleasant for you to keep quiet than to make any noise." One of the men took her arm, and, in the darkness, led her (she knew not whither) for a considerable distance, and then came to a halt. In a short time she was lifted upon a horse in front of one of her captors, and the word was given to proceed.

On through the forest, up the mountain side, over rocks and through underbrush, the little cavalcade wended its way, until Katharine could begin to distinguish through the bandage the breaking of the day. Thus far she had maintained a strict silence, knowing full well the futility of any protestation she might make; but now she asked what was meant by their carrying her off in this manner, away from her old and infirm parents, and what evil thing she had done to be thus treated?

The only answer she received was to be lifted from the horse and led down what seemed to her an almost endless stairway. At the bottom they stopped, a door grated on its hinges, opened, and shut again, as she was ushered into what she found to be a subterranean room of about ten feet square. A lamp was burning on a table in the centre. A lounge, upholstered in damask, stood in one corner, while in a recess was a small library filled with books. The room also contained three or four chairs.

Alone, and not knowing where she was, the thoughts which came into her mind were far from being of a consoling nature. She knew that her parents would be almost distracted by her sudden and unaccountable disappearance and that, at their age, it might have a fatal issue. But she also knew there was no use in whining and weeping over the matter, and she therefore determined to make the best of her surroundings and wait patiently for deliverance. Katharine was not of the whimpering and weeping kind; but of that nature which rises to the occasion as the difficulties become greater, and the obstacles seem more insurmountable. She saw no one for some hours, and then a small colored girl was let in by the outside guardian of her prison. She carried some refreshments on a server, which she placed upon the table. There were some fruit, a loaf of bread, and a small bottle of wine. Though her appetite was not of the best, she knew that for the sake of her health and strength she must eat and drink too. She therefore ate of the fruit sparingly and drank a small glass of the wine.

She tried to find out from the young African who had brought her there and what was the cause of her incarceration? But she might just as well have interrogated the walls of the cavern. She was either an idiot or else had been told to keep her mouth closed and was obeying that injunction to the letter, for Katharine could not get one word from her, good or bad. She therefore gave it up.

The little girl had been inside but a short time when a rap was heard at the door, and she grasped the server and was let out by the unseen sentinel.

Several days and nights must have passed before Katharine saw any human being except the colored attendant. There was no way of distinguishing day from night, as no ray of sunshine ever penetrated her gloomy abode. This confinement became very monotonous, and, at times, tears of sorrow for her suffering parents and friends would moisten the eyes of the captive.

The little library was a great relief to her and she spent most of the time in reading the books it contained and which had been selected with great good taste, comprising the best works of the day both in fact and fiction. But her thoughts were constantly reverting to the loved ones at home who knew not whether she was dead or alive, and this worried her more than anything else.

It was probably a week after she had arrived there that Katharine heard a heavy footstep outside. The key grated in the lock, the door swung back on its rusty hinges, and the tory chief entered the room. He was dressed with extra care. His buckskin breeches and leggings were new and bright, a fine broadcloth coat covered his person, and a broad silk crimson sash was coiled around his waist. With a low and courtly bow he saluted the captive maiden. Without returning his salutation she arose from the chair upon which she had been sitting and fastened her eyes upon him with a look full of disdain and defiance.

"My dear Miss Onderdonk," said Claudius, "I am sorry to have discommoded you, but I was compelled to it, as it was the only way in which I could be assured of your society and be certain of an uninterrupted conversation with you. The times are uncertain and tempestuous, the country is overrun by armed bands, and so under the circumstances, it was the best I could do. I hope you will forgive me!" "Claudius Smith!" said she, "if manhood or honor had any part in your constitution, the blush of shame would now mantle your cheek! You have used your power to carry off and incarcerate a defenseless woman, when you knew her friends, and especially those who are strong enough to protect her were away, fighting the battles of their country. If you have a spark of honor left in your heart you will take me from this gloomy cavern and let me return to my old and decrepit parents who need my assistance every hour."

"My dear Katharine!" returned he, "If I should do as you desire, I would be deprived of your sweet company, the enjoyment of which is the one great reason of your presence here at this moment." "If," replied she, " you could understand the horror and disgust I experience in your presence, bad as you are, I believe you would take pity on me and rid me of it!"

These words angered Claudius so much that he forgot his usual cool and calculating manner; and rising, he stepped toward Katharine as if to lay his hands upon her. Before he could reach her, however, she drew a small dagger from her bosom and raising it aloft, said: "Come one step nearer, and I shall plunge this into my heart! If you thought to wreak your vengeance on me, you may; but it will be only on my dead body! The daughter of a patriot and the sister of one of the sons of liberty, does not fear death and would embrace it a thousand times, rather than submit to dishonor!" Her eyes flashed fire, and her whole demeanor told Claudius that she was not to be trifled with. He therefore retreated to his seat near the door of the cavern. "Well," said he, rising, "I will leave you for the present, hoping that at some future time, you may be in better humor." "Go," said she! "your presence lends an added horror to this imprisonment."

At a signal the door opened and Claudius passed out leaving Katharine alone, a prey to her own bitter reflections on her present condition, and the faint prospect of her friends ever discovering the place of her confinement.

The place where she was imprisoned was situated in the roughest and least frequented part of the Ramapo mountain range several miles from the big cavern where the cowboys had their headquarters. One might pass a thousand times within a few feet of the mouth of this cave and not discover it. It was so completely hidden by bunches of mountain laurel which grew around the entrance that it would be a mere accident if it was found.

As Claudius stepped out he said to the sentinel: "See to it that she is provided with plenty of food and look out that no prowling mountain hunter discovers the place." "All right," replied the man, "I will be careful."

The tory chief struck off into a mountain path leading to the east. After following it for about a quarter of a mile he came to a small log cabin almost hidden by the dense foliage of beech and hemlock which surrounded it. As he entered he was greeted by an old negress of perhaps eighty years.

"Ise so glad you come," said she, "Ise bin lookin' for you a good while." "Well, what can I do for you, Aunt Sue?" said Claudius, as he sat down upon the only chair in the little room. "I 'spec a little money will come good. Ise done spent mos' all you lef' me de udder time; an' de young gal ober in de cave dar mus' hab something to eat," replied the aged African. "That is right, Aunt Sue," answered he, "I want you to fix up things nicely for her while she stays with us, and be sure to send it to her regularly." Claudius took a handful of coin from his pocket and threw it into the old woman's lap, saying, "There, aunty, I guess there will be enough to last until I come again." "Yes," said she, "I tink so; and now I mus' send de little one off to de store agin." "The little one" spoken of by the old negress was the colored attendant of Katharine, who also lived with the old woman in the little log house.

The tory captain now left the cabin and took a path leading down the western side of the range. He followed this path until it brought him out into the Ramapo valley about a mile north of Man of War

Rock. He then continued up the valley, following the east bank of the Ramapo river for half a mile more, which brought him in sight of his father's tavern, when he came to a halt. From this point he could get a good view of the premises. It was some time before he ventured further, but when he had satisfied himself that the coast was clear, he took a short cut across the meadow and went to the house.

It had become necessary for him to use caution as he had become in a measure a marked man, and many were on the lookout to capture him. His many crimes and depredations (as noted before) had aroused the country and made it dangerous for him to appear in the settled portions of the district without a sufficient force at his back to protect him. But on this occasion, being sure that everything was quiet, he boldly entered his father's house.

Some time had passed since he had visited them and the old people received him with every appearance of joy. To tell the truth, and, as the old saying has it, "to give the devil his due," Claudius had always been to them an affectionate son. Though he had committed many a cruel deed, at heart he was not one of those who gloated over and relished these actions. It must be admitted that circumstances had something to do with his bad reputation, and that if those circumstances had been different, Claudius also might have led a different life.

When the war broke out, he was no doubt honestly in favor of and an upholder of the policy of the King and Parliament. But being born and brought up in a neighborhood which happened to be intensely patriotic, and his family being one out of a hundred to espouse the cause of King George, he and they, were no doubt more or less persecuted for opinion's sake. His disposition therefore became in a manner soured, and he began that predatory warfare, which, in after years, made his name a synonym for all that was treacherous and cruel.

Nature had not been niggardly in her favors to Claudius. His frame was of iron, his intellect was above the average, and all who knew him had to acknowledge that his was the perfection of manly beauty.

As he entered the house he met his mother and throwing his arms around her neck, imprinted a kiss upon her wrinkled cheek. "How have you fared this long time, mother?" said he. "I have often wished to see you all, but business has kept me from it!" "Oh! I have often longed to see you, my boy; and many a sleepless night have I spent thinking of you; but I suppose you cannot always come when you would like to," replied his mother.

"That is true; business is sometimes imperative and must be attended to when duty calls," said Claudius. "Has Cobus been here lately?" asked he. "No," answered his mother, "but we are expecting him to-night. We heard from him yesterday, as one of your men passed here, and he told us he had seen him near King's Ferry in the morning and that we might expect him home to-night." "I hope he will come," said Claudius, "as I wish to consult with him on some important business."

It was quite late in the evening when a rap was heard at the door, and on opening it Cobus walked in. "Good evening all!" said Cobus, and as he saw the tory leader, he cried: "Hello, Claudius! you here? So those noble patriots have not yet caught you, eh?" "No," replied he, "not yet; though they have given me more than one close chase thus far I have eluded them."

After partaking of a supper prepared by their mother, the cowboy chief and Cobus retired to an inner room for consultation.

"Cobus," said his brother, "you know I suppose, that the Whigs and traitors hereabout, are determined to disperse and destroy our band at all hazards." That arch traitor Washington, it is said, is interesting himself in the matter, and has given positive orders to annihilate us, no matter what number of men it shall take or what it may cost. Now, from henceforth, it stands us in hand to move with the greatest caution; and what we do, must be done with the greatest secrecy. Thus far we have been very successful in all our undertakings. What the future may have in store for us, is hard to determine, but with our tried and true men the bulk of whom have proved themselves loyal to us in many a close and desperate skirmish, we ought to be able to accomplish a great deal, not only for ourselves, but for the cause we have espoused."

"Yes," answerd Cobus, "what you say is true, but that love escapade of yours, I mean the abduction of old Onderdonk's daughter has aroused a bitter and desperate feeling against us, not only in her immediate family, but throughout the whole district and her brother will no doubt, just as soon as his other duties will permit, not leave a stone unturned to find her and take vengeance on her captors.

"They do not know certainly who accomplished that job," said Claudius. "No," said Cobus, "they do not know, but they have good reason to suspect, for they know that you were one of her suitors and are really the only one who would dare to abduct her." "Well let that pass," returned Claudius, "and let them suspect whom they like. I am ready to take the chances of their vengeance."

"Cobus," said Claudius, "there lives about five miles west of the Hudson, an old and wealthy farmer by the name of Van der Blum, who owns a large herd of cattle, besides numerous horses. I think it is practicable for us to make a descent on his premises, and capture them. I would like to have it done without causing bloodshed, but in any case we must try to get them, because it will be a very easy matter to run them into the British lines and get well paid for our trouble. The attack must be made at night and then we can get them to their destination before morning and thus escape the scouting parties who are watching every movement made."

Thus were these brothers in iniquity concocting another dastardly scheme to rob their neighbors.

CHAPTER XIV.

After the abduction of Katharine, Black George was ill at ease. He went about his daily duties on the farm with a gloomy countenance and at times seemed so much preoccupied as not to notice what took place about him. "Mas' Onderdonk," said he one day, addressing the old gentleman, "I would jis like ter go huntin' fer a spell. De work on de farm ain't in bad shape now, and my 'pinion am dat dar am some deer in de mountain dis fall and if you can spar me dis nigger would jist like to take a trip. If you tink you can say yes, I'll fix up de ole rifle and git up in de mornin' airly and start."

George was aware of his master's fondness for venison and had broached the subject by a shrewd mention of that dainty, and he also knew that the loss of his daughter had made the old man more indulgent to those around him than ever before. So when he received the expected permission he immediately set about preparing for the hunt. He cleaned the old smooth bore rifle, moulded some bullets and was ready to start by day break.

Black George, though he had made hunting the excuse for wishing a vacation, had other business in mind beside that ; and as he journeyed alone, he thus communed with himself. "Dis nigger am goin' ter hunt, but not fer deer and sich like. I is tarmined to find out what dey've done wid my young missus if it takes de hull week. Dey've got her some whar in dese mountains, dat am sartin, and I mus' lay some plan ter find out whar dey've kep' her. De fust thing I mus' do am ter go an' see ole Aunt Hester up dar in Call Holler. Dey do say dat she kin tell whar ter find whats bin los', an' I belieb I'll try her."

It was toward evening when George reached Call Hollow and came in sight of the old log house and home of Aunt Hester, the fortune teller. He was, like most of his race, very superstitious, and when he knocked at the door, his hand trembled with excitement. He had heard, as who had not, of the old woman's strange and myterious power and he looked upon her as being something greater and several degrees higher than the generality of mortals. George knocked several times before there was any answer, but the door finally opened slowly, and in a cracked voice the old crone asked, what was wanted.

"I'se come ter ask you some questions about something I'se los'," said George. "Come in then," said she. "But what makes you think I can tell you where to find what you have lost?" "O, I don't know edzactly, but I heerd you could," replied George. "Well, have you any money? for unless you have, the secret cannot be revealed," continued the old lady. This question caused the negro to wince, as he had very little money, and what he did have, he hated terribly to part with. Finally, after deep reflection, he admitted he had a few shillings.

"I must have silver or the charm will not work," said Aunt Hester. "Any how, it's got to be done, and if I mus', den I mus," said George, as he laid a silver shilling in her hand. "Now sit down on this chair and tell me what you have lost," said she, as she sat down opposite to where George was sitting. He then related to the old fortune teller the story of Katharine's disappearance and gave her all the particulars he remembered of the sad affair, winding up with the assertion : "We can't find her no whar."

Aunt Hester sat for some time as though in deep thought. Her eyes were closed, and her whole appearance seemed as one in a trance. Suddenly she straightened up, opened her eyes and said : "She is locked up in a small cavern in these mountains. Two men, obeying the orders of another, took her from her home and carried her some distance and then placed her on a horse, and before daybreak, shut her in this cave, where she is still. There is a path, but little used, that leads to the top of the ridge where an old and blasted hemlock stands! Not far from the tree, there is a little cabin and the persons who live in that can tell you where she is. Find that hemlock with a dead and lightning splintered top and you will not be far from your young missus."

This being all the information he could get from the old woman, George took his departure and went in quest of the path that led to the old tree at the top of the ridge. He kept along the base of the mountain, scanning closely everything that looked like a path in the right direction until it got too dark to distinguish anything. He then prepared to camp out, a not unusual thing for him on his hunting expeditions. Finding a secluded place under an overhanging rock against the mountain side, he was soon sleeping soundly, oblivious to all things earthly.

The next morning he arose bright and early, and after partaking of a frugal breakfast of bread and cheese which he had carried in his hunting pouch, he again began his search. Still following the mountain base toward the northeast he finally struck an almost imperceptable trail, which seemed to lead up the mountain side and toward a point which, in his own mind, he thought must be the right direction. Turning into it he followed it for a considerable distance and until it brought him out upon a table rock of some extent where he could get a view, not only of the country beneath him, but also a long stretch of the ridge above.

He stopped there to reconnoitre and find his bearings. Toward the south and east the beautiful and fruitful valleys of the Hackensack and

Pascack stretched out, while toward the north and west his view was limited by the long range of the Ramapo hills and the rugged peaks of Verdritige Hook stretching almost from where he stood to the precipitous rock which juts far out into the waters of the Hudson.

While standing there his eyes wandered over the range toward the north, and he was just about starting on the path again when all at once he caught a glimpse of a huge hemlock whose naked branches were outlined against the sky, far up on the summit of the ridge above him. Grasping his rifle tighter, and thinking of the old fortune teller's description, Black George, with renewed energy, continued the ascent.

The distance was greater than it seemed as there was more than one intervening precipice and rocky gorge which it was necessary to flank or avoid. But he trudged on, saying to himself: "Dat ole woman done tole de truth, I'se sure! Dat am de tree wid de dead lims at de top, de same as she tole me. Oh! lor' a massy! if dis nigger kin only fine out whar dey am keepen her, wont ole Mas' Onderdonk an' Captain Rem. be glad?"

At last the path brought him to the summit and very near the great hemlock. There it stood just as the dame of Call Hollow had described it—a large thunder-riven tree, whose topmost branches had been blasted by the lightning's flash, and whose giant proportions made it the monarch of the mountain. And there also, not more than a hundred yards from it, stood the little cabin, a diminutive log house, which George recognized at once, from the description given by Aunt Hester.

He kept back out of sight as much as possible, in the thick undergrowth of the forest, and made up his mind to watch the cabin and find out whether the occupants had any visitors. It was nearly noon when he reached the summit of the mountain and he had been concealed about an hour, when from his hiding place he saw a man enter the log house. He was heavily armed, and dressed in half military and half hunting costume, a three-cornered hat, and a buckskin hunting jacket, and breeches, and a crimson scarf or sash was wound around his waist. This dress showed that he belonged to some band of irregulars, who fought on their own hook, and was a certain sign, in George's estimation, that he was one of the tory gang of Claudius.

George continued to watch until the man came out of the house, followed by a little colored girl, and together they started in a westerly direction from the house. The girl had a small basket in her hand while the man carried a pitcher of water, or some other liquid. The negro crawled out of his hiding place and followed the pair as best he could without being seen. He kept them in sight for about five minutes, when, in a twinkling, they both disappeared. "Well, now den! don't dat beat all?" said George to himself. "Dey mus a gone ker chuck, into de ground! But jis wait. Dis darkey am bound fer to fine de hole whar dey gone in, if it takes de hull day." And as he said this he sat down in a clump of bushes to await their reappearance.

It was near a bunch of laurel where he had lost sight of them and it was this spot that he kept his eye upon. He did not have long to wait, for in a few minutes a little black head arose as it were from behind the bush and its owner tripped lightly back along the path leading to the log cabin.

George now determined to get close enough to the spot to make sure what kind of a place it was, and getting down on his hands and knees, he crawled toward the place as carefully as he could.

It was sometime before he got there, as he did not wish to be seen from the cabin, and more than that, he did not know how many more armed men were hidden about. After considerable labor, he reached the spot, and raising himself to his feet, saw just behind the laurel bush the entrance to the cavern. Quietly dropping upon his hands and knees again, he crawled away as silently as possible, and was soon out of sight and hearing from the cabin and its inmates.

"Oh glory!" said George, when he got far enough away. "I foun' de spot fer sartin! Dat am de place dey've got her shut in. An' if we don't make dem fellers sorry fer dat job, den my name ain't George." Occasionally thinking aloud in the manner noted above, he took the shortest road for home, and arrived there just as darkness closed in around the Onderdonk homestead.

Of course, his first business was to report what he had discovered to old Martinus and the rest of the family, and then to make arrangements to inform Rem. also. He was believed to be with his company between Tappan and King's Ferry and George was dispatched early the next morning to find him, and tell the good news.

The discovery George had made in the mountains created quite a commotion in the neighborhood, and several of the inhabitants volunteered to aid in rescuing Katharine from the power of the outlaws. But as nearly all the able-bodied men were enlisted in the service of their country, the main dependence must be placed upon Rem, and such of his company as could be spared to accompany him.

George found Rem on the borders of Quashpeake Lake, and most of his company scattered along that part of the Hudson immediately east of the lake. He was highly elated when he heard George relate what he had discovered, and though he was not entirely certain that the person imprisoned in the cavern was his sister, he had good reason to believe it to be she. "In any case," said Rem, "they have some one shut up there, and it is our duty to liberate whoever it may be."

He gathered about him a dozen or more of his men, and leaving Dirck in command of the remainder, started forthwith for the mountains. By a forced march they arrived the next night at the foot of the hills where the path discovered by George led up to the summit. They halted here temporarily, to give the men a rest. When darkness had fairly set in, George, at the command of Rem, took the lead, and with the rest following in single file began the ascent. In silence, each man following in the footsteps of the other, they slowly and cautiously wended their way to the summit and arrived at the foot of the blasted hemlock near midnight. There they remained until daylight began to streak the eastern sky, when, still led by the faithful negro, they quietly surrounded the mouth of the cavern. So silently had they come that even the sentinel had not discovered their presence.

At a motion from Rem. the men brought their rifles to a present, and while thus prepared he picked up a fragment of rock and threw it into the entrance to the cavern. It could be heard tumbling from one rocky step to another, until it landed at the bottom.

At once a noise as of startled footsteps was heard, and up rushed the sentinel, (who no doubt had been quietly sleeping), only to look into the muzzles of a dozen rifles, held dangerously near his head. "Surrender!" shouted Rem, in a voice that resounded through the rocky ravines and came echoing back in a hundred different tones. The sentinel seeing there was no help for it quietly delivered his rifle and other arms, and was placed in charge of two of the company. "Hand over the key to this infernal hole in the rocks!" demanded Rem; "that I may set at liberty whoever is confined therein!"

Taking the key, and followed closely by Black George, Rem. led the way down the incline to the doorway of the prison. Unlocking the heavy door which guarded the entrance, he swung it back, and stepped into the room. There sat Katharine, near a table and in an attitude of defiance as though she expected to again meet her persecutor. She was completely dazed and for a moment seemed almost struck dumb.

"My dear sister!" cried Rem, "do you not know me?" As he said this, she sprang into his arms. "Oh Rem!" was all she could utter, as her head dropped upon his shoulders, and she burst into tears! "Oh Rem! have you come at last? I have looked for you so long!" said she as she still clung about his neck. "Yes, my dear Katharine, I have come to set you free, but we all have this faithful friend to thank for finding out where you were confined." Thus saying, he pushed George forward into the light. "But for his persevering shrewdness, we might never have found you." "Why, George, how can I ever thank you enough or repay you for this?" said Katharine. "You paid me a hundred times fore now, Miss Katharine," replied he. "I is only glad ter git you out ob dis awful place." "Come, let us get away from this miserable hole," said Rem, and taking his sister's arm, led her out into the free mountain air.

"Oh, Rem!" said she, "I feel as though in another world and I do not know how to be grateful enough for getting me out of that lonesome and gloomy place. Though I have not been ill treated or abused by my captors, still the suffering in mind I have endured through these long and dreary weeks of imprisonment, almost drove me insane. The thought that my friends were ignorant of the place of my confinement and that the chances of ever being able to find it were few and distant, worried me terribly! How are father and mother, Rem? Oh! I have thought so much about them, and how they suffered in mind, on account of my absence that for many nights I did not close my eyes to sleep." "Of course, they were almost crazed at first, but on account of the encouragement of friends and myself, they have borne up under this affliction better than could have been expected," replied Rem.

The journey down the mountain was very trying to Katharine, as in her imprisonment nearly all exercise had been denied her; but the anticipation of soon meeting her parents and friends again nerved her for the effort and when they arrived at the base of the mountain she insisted on continuing the journey on foot to her home. They therefore continued on, and reached their destination early in the evening of the same day.

There was great rejoicing in the old mansion where for some time there had been nothing but bitter sorrow, and the old people seemed to take on a new lease of life now, that their beloved daughter had been returned to them, almost as one raised from the dead. Katharine's bosom friend, Mary Demaray, had, during the whole time of her absence, acted the part of a daughter to the old people. She visited them daily, and by many little attentions and in every way encouraging them by her hopeful and cheering conduct had kept up their spirits under their sad and terrible affliction.

Leaving Katharine at home in the bosom of her family and among friends whose love she prized, we will follow Captain Rem. on his return to the borders of Lake Quashpeake near the banks of the Hudson. Though it was hard to break away from the joyful and reunited family, the call to duty was imperative, and Rem. and his men set out immediately for their scouting ground.

CHAPTER XV.

Captain Rembrandt Onderdonk and his little company were on their way to the scenes of their duty and had just passed through a small piece of wood land and were about to cross a meadow two miles west of their destination, when one of his men discovered a British officer alone under a tree on the opposite side. The young scout who had made the discovery had recently purchased a new rifle and had had no opportunity to test its qualities up to this time. He therefore determined to try it now. It was a long shot, but lying down on the ground he rested the piece over one of the rails of a fence near by, and taking a long and true aim, fired! The unfortunate officer dropped stone dead, shot through the heart. He belonged to a detachment lying just over the ridge and near the Hackensack river.

It may be said, and truely too, that such actions did not come within the bounds of civilized warfare, but the burning of Closter, the massacre of

Colonel Baylor and his troops at Old Tappan and the murder of many old and decrepit men by the tories and British soldiers, had aroused such a bitter and revengeful feeling throughout the land that many things were done now, and thought to be fair retaliation, which, but for them, would have been condemned by all. After this incident they struck off to the north for the purpose of avoiding the British pickets who were stationed quite a distance up the Hackensack valley. They had got almost to the end of their journey when Captain Rem. was notified by one of his men, who had remained behind when the expedition was sent to liberate his sister, that the cowboys would that night attack the Van der Blum place, which was located about three miles west of where they were. The scout had made the discovery while patroling the country just north of the Van der Blum farm. He saw the gang, or a part of them in concealment in a thicket about a mile from the place to be attacked, and had overheard them discussing their plans.

Captain Onderdonk immediately determined to frustrate their designs if possible. For that purpose he gave orders to his men to proceed to the place separately and to keep under cover as much as they could. They all got there unseen by every one except the family. The old farmer was highly pleased to receive such a reinforcement at such a critical time, and treated the men to everything the place afforded. The scouts were secreted in the dwelling and in a short time were prepared to receive the marauders.

Just as the last ray of daylight disappeared in the west, the cowboys emerged from the forest about a quarter of a mile north of the house. About half of them, obeying the orders of their leader, proceeded to collect the herd of some twenty cattle which were pasturing in the meadows between the woodland and the barns, while the other half came directly to the barn. Without pretending to ask the consent of the owner, they went into the barn and in a very short time brought out the horses, tethered them together, and were ready to move away.

They had just passed the house, believing themselves secure from interruption by the old couple and the few female servants they knew to be in their employ, not even taking the trouble to investigate whether there might not be some others there, when into their rear was poured a withering fire, which either killed or wounded nearly half of the band. Before they recovered from their astonishment, Rem. and his men rushed out, and before the cowboys could rally and return the fire, another volley was sent into their ranks.

"Now for them!" cried Rem, as he ordered his men to use the bayonet! "Give it to them boys!" And with a rush they were upon them with the naked steel. The cowboys could not stand before this onslaught, and took to their heels, except those who were too badly wounded or lay dead upon the ground. As they were running away, several of them turned and fired, but with little effect, as only one of the defenders was wounded.

During the fray, Rem. hunted for Claudius with the savageness of a tiger after its prey, but he was not to be found as the expedition was commanded by his brother Cobus. Having left their dead and wounded on the ground, it became the duty of

Rem. and his men to bury the dead and to care for those who had received injuries. The wounded men had their wounds dressed, and the next morning the dead (five in number) were buried at the edge of the forest. The wounded, to the number of four, were left at the farm house in charge of four of Rem's company until they were strong enough to be disposed of as prisoners.

After attending to this part of the business the remainder of the company left for the lake. This fortunate intervention of Captain Onderdonk and his scouts saved the old farmer an amount of property whose loss would have seriously crippled him for years, and he gratefully acknowledged his indebtedness to the scouts for their opportune arrival on the scene.

CHAPTER XVI.

The war, which had been dragging along for nearly five years, was still being prosecuted with varying success by both sides. At times, the King's forces were successful and everything looked dark for the patriot cause, and then again the American arms would triumph, and cause rejoicing throughout the land, and a consequent depression in the feelings of those who sympathized with the King and Parliament.

One of the most depressing and terrible blows the cause of liberty had yet received, occurred during the latter part of this year 1780. General Arnold, through interceding with Washington, had obtained the command of the fortress at West Point on the Hudson, at that time the most important post in America. He then proposed to Sir Henry Clinton, the British commander at New York, to surrender the post and Major John Andre, the Adjutant General of the British army, was sent to confer with him on that subject. He ascended the river in the Vulture, an English sloop of war, landed near West Point, and at midnight met and had a conference with the traitor, at what has since been designated as the Treason House near the village of Haverstraw and which was then owned by one Joshua Hett Smith.

Andre's intention was, after the conference was ended, to again board the Vulture and return in her to New York. But while he was on shore Captain Onderdonk's company of scouts which was patrolling the west bank of the Hudson at that point, opened fire on the vessel, and she dropped down the river. Morning dawned before they had completed their plans and Andre was left within the American lines. He then determined to cross the river and return to New York that way. He reached Tarrytown in safety, but there he was arrested by three militiamen named Paulding, Williams and Van Wart, who searched him, and finding papers on his person which led them to believe he was a spy they took him to the nearest military post. Though he attempted to bribe them in every way, these incorruptible patriots, though poor and needy, refused his offer, and conducted him to Colonel Jamison.

Andre was finally taken across the river to Tappan and there imprisoned in the Yost Mabie house, since known as the Seventy-six House, until he could be tried as a spy. Captain Barent Van Houten and his company, after the capture of Stony Point, had been on duty at Fort Sidman and the different fortifications in Ramapo Pass, but were now ordered to Tappan to act as a guard around the prison of Major Andre. On their way there they stopped at the Van Houton home for a rest. Old Rulof received them with gladness, and set before them everything in the shape of refreshments that the house afforded.

While in the old neighborhood Barent took advantage of the occasion to call upon his betrothed. He found Mary in a cheerful mood, as her particular friend Katharine Onderdonk had just been rescued from the tory gang of Claudius, and the great rejoicing in the neighborhood on account of that event made his visit there a pleasant occasion.

In the afternoon Barent and Mary, together

with Lieutenant Bertholf of his company, made a call at the Onderdonk mansion. They found the family in good spirits. The new barns and outbuildings replacing those burned by the cowboys were about completed, and to cap the climax of their joys, their only daughter was in their midst once more. The afternoon was one of the loveliest of the season, and the clear bracing September air was most invigorating.

The young Lieutenant with Katharine on his arm, and Barent and his betrothed following, spent the afternoon in rambling through the orchards and about the farm, and enjoyed the balmy weather and the society of one another to the fullest extent. The early frost had painted the mountains with all the colors of the rainbow. The crimson of the maple, the russet brown of the oak, the scarlet and purple of the sumac, together with the dark green of the laurel and hemlock, made it a fairy scene far beyond description or the power of the most cunning artist's pencil.

By the time they arrived from their ramble in the fields, Barent and Mary noticed that Lieutenant Bertholf was in great danger of being captured and made a prisoner by the intelligent conversation and captivating manners of the lovely sister of Captain Rem. It was also apparent that Katharine seemed to enjoy the society of the young lieutenant immensely.

Lieutenant Henry Bertholf came of a solid old Dutch family from beyond the mountains in this same county of Orange, a family whose name had been associated with and was prominent among the early settlers of that part of the Province of New York. In the early part of the war he, as well as all the other members of the family, had espoused the cause of the Colonies and had, since then, taken an active part in the struggle. Henry had walked down to Fort Sidman and enlisted as a private, but by good conduct and especially by great bravery shown in the desperate attack on, and capture of the fort at Stony Point, he had been promoted to a lieutenancy. He was about the medium height, straight as an arrow, with deep-set flashing gray eyes overhung by a broad and intellectual brow. He certainly had no reason to quarrel with dame nature in regard to his personal appearance.

But this dalliance with love and beauty could not continue, so after taking leave of the old folks and bidding a sweet good bye to the young ladies, Barent and the young lieutenant took their departure and at the head of their company continued the march to Tappan.

They arrived there near noon of the next day, went into camp and part of their men were immediately detailed to guard the unfortunate young officer confined in the old stone tavern. The capture of Major Andre and the opportune arrival of Washington at West Point saved the post from falling into the hands of the British; but Arnold being apprised through the stupidity of Colonel Jamison, escaped, eventually got on board of the Vulture and lived to reap the base reward of his treachery —a commission as Colonel in the British army and the sum of six thousand three hundred and fifteen pounds sterling.

Washington appointed a board of fourteen military officers to try Andre, who, after hearing his confession, (for he was too conscientious to deny the part he had taken in the matter), unanimously convicted him of being a spy, and, according to the law of nations, condemned him to death upon the scaffold. During his confinement he won the love and respect of all whose duties brought them near his person and especially of Captain Barent Van Houten and the officers and men of his company who had been detailed to guard his prison.

It was on the morning of the 2d of October, 1780, when the beating of the reveille awoke the soldiers of the guard at Tappan and ushered in the day of doom for Major John Andre, the British spy. The sun rose in all the glory of an October morning, and its first rays, as they glinted over the rocky barrier of the Palisades, penetrated through the iron bars and lighted up the cell of the doomed man. There was scarcely one who knew him who did not deprecate the stern necessity of war and wish it could be otherwise in his case. The doom of a spy is death, and every soldier knows it; and when he ventures within the enemy's lines he is certain of the penalty if taken. But if some mercy had been shown to Captain Nathan

Hale, who knows whether Major John Andre might not have been spared?

Washington offered to exchange Andre for Arnold but Sir Henry Clinton refused. He even set a plan on foot to capture the arch traitor that he might have an excuse to pardon Andre, but this plan miscarried, and Sergeant John Champe, in consequence, served a hard apprenticeship in the British army for his daring attempt to capture the traitor.

Andre had petitioned Washington to be shot as a soldier instead of being hung like a common criminal. The Commander-in-Chief, moved by his appeal, presented the request to his officers, but it was refused. Finding that there was no alternative, he became submissive to his fate and calmly prepared for death.

Captain Van Houten's company was ordered under arms and formed in front of the prison. Lieutenant Bertholf entered the old tavern, and proceeding to the room in which he was confined, informed Andre that the hour for his execution had arrived. **He had** already prepared himself **for the summons and** said he was ready for the ordeal. The lieutenant escorted him to the front of the building where the soldiers were in line, ready for the march to the gallows. This had been erected on the hill west of the little village, probably a quarter of a mile distant. Placing him between two ranks of soldiers the order was given to advance; and he began his last journey on earth, which was to end at the scaffold.

Solemnly, and with muffled drums beating, the detachment wended its way up the hill. Lieutenant Bertholf walked by his side the whole distance and the only complaint he made was as to the manner of his death. "I had hoped to die the death of a soldier," said he, "but the fortunes of war have denied me that boon, and I must be content!"

Arriving at the gallows the company formed a hollow square about it. The condemned man was placed in a wagon and when the word was given, it was drawn from beneath him and the victim was left dangling in the air.

Thus perished as a spy Major John Andre, Adjutant-General of the British army, who under other, and more favorable circumstances, might have lived to be an ornament to his country. Through the infamy and base treachery of one who had been honored and confided in by the nation this noble young man died a shameful death on the gallows.

He was buried near the spot where he was executed and his remains rested there until 1821, when, by the orders of the Duke of York, his body was disinterred and carried to England, and his remains now repose in Westminster Abbey, that Pantheon of England's honored dead. After the execution, the company returned to camp at Tappan, where Washington then had his headquarters.

CHAPTER XVII.

Upon the highest point of Torne mountain, the loftiest peak of the Ramapo range, and which overlooks the valley of the Ramapo for many miles, might have been seen on a pleasant morning in October, 1780, a man with a small field glass closely scanning the valley around Fort Sidman. He seemed to be intently watching something that was taking place in the immediate vicinity of the fort. After looking through the glass for some minutes, he turned and said to a companion who was sitting on the branching roots of a huge elm a short distance behind him : "Cobus, there is a great commotion at the fort, and from what I can observe, it looks as though an expedition is being fitted out for some purpose. Take a look through the glass, and see what you can make of it!"

After looking through the glass Cobus replied : "Yes, there appears to be something more than common going on, and I think, with you, that a body of soldiers is about to move from the fort. Yes, now I see them moving and I believe they mean to march south. Look for yourself, Claudius, and see if it is not so?"

Claudius, for it was none other, took the glass from his brother's hand, and looked steadily through it for some time. As he lowered it he replied: "Yes, they are moving south, and I have no doubt are bound for the Jersies. Well, let them go and it may be that some of them will never get back, for I think there will be some warm work in that direction before long." "At any rate," said Cobus, "they are not moving in the direction to give us any trouble, and that is some satisfaction."

"That is true," remarked Claudius, "and while the garrison here is only strong enough to man the works and protect the Pass, we can do some profitable business for ourselves." "There is only one party we have to fear and that is the company of scouts under that infernal Rem. Onderdonk," said Cobus. "You are right there," said his brother, "they are more troublesome to us than the whole rebel army combined."

From the summit of Torne mountain, where these two worthies stood, could be had one of the finest views of mountain, valley and woodland to be found in the country. To the north could be seen the two mountain ranges that bound the valley on either side, until they slope down to the fertile fields in the far distance. To the south the eye took in the level lowlands and gently rolling hills of the whole stretch of country almost to the city of New York. To the east might be seen the rugged peaks of Verdrietige Hook and the entire County of Orange south of the mountains, bounded only by the Highlands of the Hudson and the hills of Westchester; while beneath through the whole length of the valley glided the silver waters of the Ramapo.

To the lover of nature in her different moods, here was a study of wondrous diversity and beauty; but whether these two brothers either realized or enjoyed this grand scenery is beyond our ken.

"Come Cobus, let us find the boys and see what arrangement can be made," said Claudius, as he turned and took the path down the mountain to the north, followed by Cobus.

In a small **and** secluded valley, about a mile north of Torne mountain, were gathered a band of about twenty men. They were dressed in **a diversity of** costumes and all were armed with **rifles which were** stacked conveniently around the camp. They seemed to have nothing particular to do, but were lounging about in all sorts of positions. Some were enjoying their pipes, some roasting meat over a fire, and **others** were lying down and seemed to be sleeping. But at the same time an observer would have noticed that several sentinels were stationed at proper distances about the camp to guard against any attempt **at** surprising it.

As the reader **has** no doubt **surmised,** this was the camp of the cowboys **and tories** under the command of Claudius Smith.

A log house of pretty fair size stood in a clump of evergreen trees and formed the neucleus about which several shanties of smaller size were built. It was about the hour **of** noon when Claudius and his brother arrived in the camp, and, calling his men around him, laid before them a scheme to rob some farms north of the mountains.

"To-night," said he, "we will make our way through the mountains to the north end of the valley and lie quiet there until darkness again makes it safe to get out into the open country, when, if our plans do not miscarry, we can, with ease and safety, run off the large herd belonging to old Gerardus Bertholf, who lives about an hour's march from the north outlet of the Pass. If nothing intervenes to prevent we can drive them down the north side of the mountain as far as Wanaque Valley, and through that to New York. It is impossible to take the shorter way by the Pass on account of the fortifications and the constant patrol of scouting parties through it."

"Prepare yourselves for business men and be ready to move at sun set," said Claudius, and turning to Cobus, he continued, "leave two good men to guard the camp until we return."

There was hurry and bustle in the camp of the cowboys. Knapsacks were packed, arms were cleaned and ammunition prepared, and when the sun disappeared behind the western hills they were ready for the march. At the word from Claudius the cowboys started, with Cobus in the lead. He was acquainted with every mountain path and with almost every rock and tree in the range.

They got to their destination about daybreak, and selecting a spot where the foliage and undergrowth were very thick, they awaited again the darkness of night.

Claudius sent one of his men out to reconnoitre and report. He returned about noon and reported that the coast was clear and that they would have no difficulty in capturing the whole herd, as they were pasturing in the meadow some distance from the house and with no one to guard them but two men and a boy. As night set in they started for the farm and in about an hour arrived there.

Quietly they gathered around the doomed herd, collecting them together with as little noise as possible. Just as they thought they had succeeded without alarming any of the household, a dog came out barking furiously, and making towards them seemed determined to lay hold of the first one he came to. This frightened one of the latest recruits of the band and he fired a pistol at the dog. Just as he fired, Claudius seized him by the throat and dashed him to the ground.

"What do you mean?" said the chief. "But for your ignorance, I would crush out your miserable life! You have brought the whole family and neighborhood upon us! Get up now and fight for your life!" said he, as he lifted the man to his feet as though he had been an infant.

Sure enough out came the old man, rifle in hand, and his two workmen, armed with hay forks. They dashed at the first one they saw, supposing the hen house was being robbed.

Claudius did not wish to shed blood if it could be avoided, but the old farmer was so impetuous that, in self defense, one of the cowboys was compelled to fire, and down went the man badly, though not mortally wounded. Seeing him fall, his two workmen took to their heels and escaped in the darkness.

Detailing about half the band to drive the cattle ahead, Claudius, with the other half covered the rear, to prevent any attack from that direction.

Leaving the farmer where he fell, they hurried away with their booty.

Before morning dawned the cowboys with the cattle were in Wanaque Valley, where they deemed themselves comparatively secure, as many of the inhabitants were sympathizers with the mother country. But beyond the valley and on the south side of the mountains, the people were in the main patriotic and many of the male population were in the American army. It was therefore necessary to use a great deal of caution after arriving at that part of the journey, and for that reason, when the mouth of the valley was reached, Claudius gave orders to halt and wait for daylight.

The old farmer, Gerardus Bertholf, though badly wounded, still thought of recovering his property, and when he found that the cowboys had taken his whole herd he determined to circumvent them, if possible.

He therefore dispatched one of his men down Ramapo Valley for the purpose of notifying Colonel Malcolm, the commander at Fort Sidman. When the man arrived at the fort he was taken immediately to the commander. He told him that no doubt the marauders had taken the road through Wanaque Valley for the purpose of driving the cattle to New York.

Colonel Malcolm saw that by sending a company of soldiers immediately to the southern mouth of the valley, they might intercept the cowboys before they passed that spot. He therefore dispatched a company of twenty men under a trusty officer for the purpose.

They took the road along the base of the eastern range and arrived at the southern outlet before the gang had passed. Concealing themselves in the bushes each side of the road they awaited their approach.

The shadows of night had scarcely fallen over hill and valley when the cowboys were heard coming down the road. About half of their men acted as an advance guard and preceded the herd which were being driven by the remainder.

On they came, thinking themselves secure from attack, until those in front had just passed the place where the soldiers were concealed. Then the order to fire rang out upon the still night air, and caused them to turn and look back. As they did so the report of twenty rifles startled the echoes and the bullets crashed into their ranks! Those in the rear closed up and awaited the onset of the soldiers. As they rushed from the bushes into the road the remaining cowboys returned the fire so effectively that the scouts were for a moment staggered. Rallying immediately, however, they charged with the bayonet directly among the enemy!

The noise and clatter of the affray frightened the cattle and caused a stampede. Helter skelter, away they went into the bushes, up the mountain side, and out into the open country, so that in a few minutes not an animal was left in the road.

The cowboys retreated very slowly up the valley and those who were not killed or wounded in front, now came back to aid their comrades.

As the soldiers were pursuing the rear guard, the others coming up now, fired a volley into their ranks which almost threw them into confusion again. But the officer in command divided his force, and, at the head of one part charged back among them! This soon ended the fight, as the cowboys fled into the mountains and left the soldiers masters of the field.

The extreme darkness of the night made the aim of the combatants uncertain and prevented a heavy loss of life; but as it was, four of the marauders were killed, and quite a large number wounded—how many could not be found out, as they carried them away in their retreat. The soldiers had three men killed and five wounded.

In the morning some of the cattle were collected, and on their return to Fort Sidman the soldiers drove them back to the Pass, where the old farmer finally recovered them. It was afterward learned that the cowboys gathered the remnant of the herd as best they could and finally got them into New York. But it was a costly job for the tory gang, and the few they eventually sold scarcely paid the expenses of the journey.

As we have noticed before, the business of these predatory bands was becoming unprofitable and very dangerous as the people were on the watch for them, and when they could be located they were pounced upon either by the scouting parties led by such men as Captain Rem. and his brother

Dirck, or by detachments from Fort Sidman and Tappan.

Still, when they reached the rocky fastnesses of the Ramapo range, they were comparatively secure. They knew every inch of the ground and it was nearly an impossibility to take them by surprise, when they had once reached these natural strongholds.

Claudius had experienced a sad disappointment when he visited the little cavern near the old hemlock again to find that the bird had flown and left the cage empty. The sentinel had been taken prisoner and turned over by Rem. to the regulars at Tappan, so there was no one to tell the tale of Katharine's rescue but the old negress and the little colored girl who occupied the log hut near the cave.

By questioning them, Claudius found out that a party of armed men had surprised the sentinel and taken Katharine away with them. Of course, Claudius was fully satisfied who had been instrumental in her rescue, and this knowledge added another grain to the weight of vengeance he was accumulating and laying up against Rem. This king of the scouts had so often stepped between him and his most cherished plans, that he now hated him with a perfect hatred and impatiently awaited the time when he could wreak his vengeance upon him to its full satisfaction.

The tory chief had met with great success at the beginning of his career and for a time he had supposed himself to be one of fortune's favored ones. Now, however, the times were greatly changed. The patriot cause was looking brighter, and on several occasions his band had been defeated when from appearances everything seemed favorable to success.

Oftentimes when alone in one of his strongholds in the mountains his thoughts would revert to that dark and stormy night when he visited the fortune teller of Call Hollow and heard from her lips that dire prophecy of what his end would be. In his own mind he would then think over recent events, and compare them with the words of the old woman ; and, imagining that some portion of the prophecy had proved true, would ask himself whether the end might not be the same?

Then again, he would, by an effort of his

strong will, throw all these gloomy **forebodings to** the winds, and appear before **his** companions **as** one of the most light hearted and careless of the **band.** But do what he would, ever and anon, the old hag's words would come back to him with increased force and as time went by the effect of these unhappy thoughts was plainly discernible. His band of reckless outlaws had been diminishing for some time and recruits were few and far between, plainly showing to others, as well as to himself, that the business was becoming unpopular.

Claudius had appeared as **one** of the most hardened, and **one** not likely to give a thought to past sins, yet now the blood of his victims seemed a heavy weight on his soul and caused him many a sleepless night.

CHAPTER XVIII.

The year 1780, had been one of many ups and downs in the cause of freedom. In the South, the city of Charleston had surrendered to the British; the battle of Hanging Rock had been won by General Sumter, and though starting into the fight with only two rounds of ammunition for each of his men, they soon filled their cartridge boxes from those of the fleeing tories.

Many times Marion and Sumter went into battle with only enough muskets for a portion of their men, but as some of them fell either killed or wounded, the remainder armed themselves with the guns of their disabled comrades and continued the fight.

At King's mountain, the independent riflemen, each company under its own leader, attacked Ferguson, who had been sent to gather and rally the tories of the neighborhood, and killed one hundred and fifty of his men, together with their leader, and took the rest prisoners.

At the battle of Camden the patriot army suffered a defeat. It was there that the chivalric Baron De Kalb, who commanded the Continental regulars, fell covered with wounds and glory, a costly sacrifice in the cause of liberty.

Before the battle began, he told his brother officers that he could not depend upon the militia; but that he was too old to run, and that his Continentals would stand by him. And so it proved; the militia fled at the first fire, and the brunt of the battle fell upon the regulars, who fought until they saw their beloved commander fall, pierced with eleven wounds, when they, too, retired, though in good order.

But the British loss in this battle was heavier than the American, and though the patriots retired and left the British masters of the field, the effect was little less injurious to them than a defeat.

About this time there was quite a large detachment of our French allies stationed just south of Ramapo Pass, under the command of Count Rochambeau. The French and American officers often met at the Suffern tavern, owned by a staunch old patriot named John Suffern, and used as a headquarters by Washington when in that neighborhood.

At one of these convivial meetings, a controversy arose between a young French and American officer which ended in a challenge being given by the Frenchman and accepted by the American. They met at a place near the base of Noorde Kup peak, just north of what is called the Point of the Mountain. At the first fire the young Frenchman fell, mortally wounded. He was buried on the banks of the Mahwah, where his remains still lie, far from his native land and the loved ones at home.

Fortunate it is that, since that day such distressing incidents have become less frequent and such false ideas of honor more unpopular in our glorious land.

Here too, in the Suffern home, was often seen Colonel Aaron Burr, then a dashing young officer in the Continental army. It was from this place that he rode many times over to Paramus to visit the beautiful Theodosia Prevost, who afterwards became his wife. Even when stationed across the river in Westchester, he was attracted by her magnetic influence, and, calling a boat's crew and with his horse tied in the boat, he would cross to Sneden's landing and ride from there fifteen miles to Paramus and back again before the first ray of sunlight lit up the eastern horizon.

All through the war Burr served his country faithfully ; but in after years, though elevated to the second place of honor in the gift of his fellow citizens, he let his ambitious designs and desire for self aggrandizement lead him into a conspiracy to establish an empire west of the Alleghanies, of which he should be the emperor, or chief. For this he was arrested and tried at the city of Richmond, but for want of proof was finally released. His after life, however, seemed embittered by this failure, and when his beloved and beautiful daughter, Theodosia, was lost at sea, he became gloomy and despondent and in his retirement was almost forgotten by his countrymen.

It was also near this place, in the valley of the Ramapo, where the great chain was made which was stretched across the Hudson at West Point to prevent British war vessels from ascending the river. The remains of many of those old furnaces and forges where it was made can yet be seen dotting this historic valley throughout its whole length. They are the fit reminders of the industry and perseverance of our forefathers, who delved from the surrounding hills their mineral treasures.

It was at the base of old Hooghe Kup, that grand sentinel which guards the southern outlet of the valley, that in 1715 the Tuscarora tribe of Indians rested for some time, on their journey from their seat in North Carolina, to join their relatives the Iroquois, or Five Nations, in Central New York.

Here in the mountains which bound the western side of the Pass, may yet be found a mixture of that race. Of course they have been mixed with white and negro blood, but some specimens may still be found of that race, which, before the white men came, were the conquerors of almost half the continent.

After remaining here for a while, they took up their march and became one of the Six Nations which afterwards became the deadly enemies of the Colonies in their struggle for independence. For several years they harassed our frontier, and almost drove the white settlers from that part of the State. At last, General Sullivan was dispatched with an army to punish them. Near where the city of Elmira now stands, he met and vanquished them and taught them a lesson they did not forget for a generation.

It was this tradition among what is left of the tribe that caused Silas Mountpleasant, a nephew of the head chief, to wander back from Lake Erie and pass the rest of his life in the shadows of the Ramapo range. For long years he was a well known member of the community residing in, or near the valley, remaining until consumption, that scourge of the red man, ended his life in the house of a great hearted neighbor, who, for several years before his death had cared for him as if one of his family.

But the red man's career is almost ended, not only in this valley, but throughout our whole broad land; and it will not be many years before they, like the bison of their plains, will be among the things which are not.

CHAPTER XIX.

The great struggle for Independence was slowly drawing to a close and the battles between the opposing forces, this year, (1781) were in almost every instance favorable to the American arms. Though the traitor Arnold had done some mischief in the burning of the city of Richmond, and some other less important places, yet at Cowpens, Guilford Court House, and Eutaw, the patriots more than held their own.

Washington, with a large part of the army, together with our French allies, making a feint as though intending to attack New York, had marched from Newburgh on the Hudson, and when within a short distance of that city swerved aside, and, by forced marches night and day, invested Cornwallis at Yorktown.

Captain Barent Van Houten and his command had been ordered to join the army on its march through the valley and were now forming a part of the besieging force.

So rapid had been the movements of the allied army, that it was some time before Sir Henry Clinton discovered their purpose and they were already besieging Cornwallis when he found that they had disappeared from his front.

Clinton at once embarked with an army of seven thousand men to go to the relief of Yorktown, but five days before his arrival there Cornwallis had surrendered his whole army of more than seven thousand men, besides an immense quantity of arms and military stores. Clinton therefore returned to New York, disappointed in his expectation of raising the siege.

The surrender of Corwallis and his well equipped army was the cause of universal joy and rejoicing to the people of the country and nothing but praises of Washington and La Fayette, Rochambeau and De Grasse, were heard throughout the land.

Soon after the surrender, the northern division of the army returned to its old position on the Hudson, which of course brought Barent and his men back again to Fort Sidman. They were received with acclamations of delight on their return. Bonfires were burned and signal lights blazed from every mountain top between the banks of the Hudson and the Delaware.

As the war was now thought to be nearly over, the dawn of peace gave opportunity to attend to other things nearer home, which had been postponed for the more pressing needs of the country at large. One of these, and the main one too, was to crush out and disperse the predatory bands of malignant tories which infested the mountain region of the southern part of New York.

To do this effectually, the company under the command of Barent Van Houten, and the scouts led by Captain Rembrandt Onderdonk, were detailed for the purpose.

Many an effort had been made before to accomplish this, but they had never proved entirely successful and the tories and cowboys still pursued their dastardly vocation of robbing and murdering the unarmed inhabitants of this district. But now, a supreme effort to destroy them was to be made, and these companies were selected on account of their superior knowledge of the part of the country in which they were to operate. These two officers, too, were thoroughly acquainted with the ground and for that reason were well adapted to lead the expedition.

The urgent need of patrolling the banks of the Hudson was now relaxed, which left Captain Rem. and his men free to join in this long cherished, though often deferred plan to drive these outlaws from their haunts.

To accomplish this business properly, it was necessary that the two officers should have a mutual understanding of the matter.

Having been notified of their selection, they met and conferred in regard to the plan to be pursued. This conference was held at the old tavern at Coe's corner, midway between King's Ferry and Fort Sidman.

Captain Onderdonk proposed that his company should begin the search at the eastern end of Verdrietige Hook mountain and scour every nook, cave and valley in that range and then take in the Kakiatt and Cheesecock hills toward the west, while Captain Van Houten and his command should start into the mountains at Fort Sidman and eventually both commands meet about midway between the two points, thus making a sweeping hunt and covering every inch of the ground for the whole distance.

This plan of campaign was agreed to by Barent and acquiesced in by their two lieutenants, Dirck, Captain Rem's brother, and Bertholf.

After talking over the details of the expedition more particularly, they separated, and repaired to their respective camps. Captain Rem. after receiving special orders to drop everything else and hunt the cowboys, sent to the old place for Black George to join him at King's Ferry and aid in the grand search for Claudius and his men.

This, of course, just suited the faithful African, who had been wishing for this opportunity. He had made so many terrible threats as to what he would do if he could only get another chance at the tories that the opportunity now offered to be in at the death of the gang, made this a red letter day in his existence.

And certainly George was not a mean recruit, for he was so thoroughly acquainted with almost every mountain path, that in this respect at least, he was far ahead of nearly every other member of Captain Rem's company.

"O, Mas' Rem! dis am jist what I'se been waiten fer," said he, when he arrived at the camp. "Dis nigger's been waiten' fer de time to come when we mus' git eben wid dat tory gang an' make dem fellers sorry fer all de debbilment dey eber done! Look out! Mas' Claud, we is comin' fer you sure dis time!"

Leaving Captain Rem. almost ready to begin the campaign against the cowboys we will take a look at the preparations being made at Fort Sidman for the same purpose.

Captain Van Houten and his efficient lieutenant began immediately on their return to get their men ready for the expedition. Every rifle was cleaned, every cartridge box was replenished, and each man's knapsack was packed with provisions for the compaign. Everything was put in order as though entering on a regular campaign against a powerful enemy. The same preparation had been made by the scouts at King's Ferry, and two days after the conference at Coe's corner, both detachments were ready to enter the mountains.

CHAPTER XX.

As the men under Captain Rem. and his brother struck into the Verdrietige Hook range, near the borders of the Hudson, he said to them :

"Let the search be thorough. Cover every inch of the ground. Beat every bush and thicket; and to him who first discovers the whereabouts of Claudius and his band I promise ten pounds in sterling silver."

Captain Onderdonk had a huge account to settle with the tory chief, a great portion of which remained still uncancelled upon the debtor side of the book. There was the burning of the barns and outbuildings on the old place ; the running off of the cattle and horses ; and, above all, and overshadowing all the rest, was the dastardly abduction of his sister Katharine. At last he hoped the time had arrived to strike a balance and close the transactions **between** them.

Ever since the breaking out of hostilities Rem. had hoped to meet Claudius face to face and settle the score with him personally; but thus far that wish had been foiled, and they had never met since the evening he saw him at his father's house. But now he thought the opportunity would come when that wish would be gratified, and he impatiently awaited the time.

There was a large tract of country to be covered in this search, and to do it successfully required considerable time and a great deal of hard and weary work. But Captain Rem's company was used to mountain fighting, and inured to all kinds of hardship. The men from Fort Sidman were unused to mountain climbing, and were not so well acquainted with the ground; but their hearts were in the work, which caused them to overcome all obstacles with a determination that knew no such word as fail.

The tory sympathizers of Claudius were now on the alert, and the expedition had scarcely entered the mountains before messengers had informed him of what was in the wind. His first thought was to disband his gang, and thus escape the punishment they had so richly deserved. **But then** he knew that himself, and most of his men, were so well known among the inhabitants of the surrounding district that eventually they would be taken, if only one or two at a time, and when there was no chance for resistance.

He therefore determined that in numbers there was strength, and that at some one of the almost impregnable locations in the mountains he would make a stand and fight it out **so** long as there was **a** man left **to stand** by him.

He, himself, and many of his men, could **no** doubt escape by leaving this part of the country altogether; but even in the heart of an outlaw there is love for the place of his birth and the associations surrounding his earlier years, which, in the most degraded and desperate, is hard to eradicate and entirely subdue.

From **King's** Ferry Claudius received notice that **his old** enemy, Rem. Onderdonk, was on the **war** path to hunt him down. He, Claudius, was not to be frightened, however, though the whole world was against him; and he certainly deserved this credit—that as **the** difficulties and dangers increased his courage rose with the occasion and made him more determined than ever to resist.

He was born among these hills; his old parents were still living; and every object that binds one to his native place was located here. He knew the ordeal was before him, and he braced himself to meet it. From boyhood he had roamed over this wild and romantic district, free as the mountain eagle; and now, to think of being driven from all the associations of his youth and manhood too, made him desperate and he resolved, if necessary, to die in the last ditch.

Claudius and his brother met at the old tavern in the nook of the mountains and there made arrangements to gather the band to defend what they considered their birthright. Their men were fighters every one, for the weak ones had long since been weeded out to make room for more solid material, and now the band was composed of the hardy, reckless men of the mountains, whom work could not weary, nor danger intimidate.

After remaining at their old home for several hours they took leave of the family and started for the camp of the outlaws, situated, as before shown, about a mile north of Torne mountain. When they arrived there they found nearly the whole band had got word of the expedition and were gathered there to await the commands of their leader. They placed implicit confidence in Claudius and recognized his superior intelligence and knowledge. As the two brothers entered the camp the men gathered around them, anxious to hear any news they might have to communicate. There were some twenty-five of them, and every man of the number could be depended upon in almost any emergency.

"Well, comrades," said the chief, "I suppose you are aware of the extraordinary efforts that are being made, not only to drive us out of the country, but to capture any or all of us and to bring us to trial on charges of robbery and murder. We have our choice of three different modes of action. One is to separate and scatter ourselves over the country and run the risk of being taken one or two at a time and be dealt with as these victorious rebels may think best. Another is, to deliver ourselves up to the authorities and supplicate for mercy. And then there is another and the last, which is to stand up like men and soldiers and fight it out as long as there is a man of us left to handle a rifle.

"I have determined to leave it to yourselves, my men, who have stood by me all these years in fair weather and foul, in sunshine and in storm, in the bloody fray, and on many a weary night march, to choose which of the three modes we had better adopt."

"Come, what is your verdict?" said Claudius, as he finished speaking.

"We will fight it out and die like men rather than run like frightened rabbits, or crawl like whipped curs to their feet!" said one and all, and throwing their caps in the air they gave three rousing cheers that made the mountain gorges ring again, and shook the foliage on the trees above.

"They have already begun the hunt," said Claudius. "They are strong in numbers, and one of the parties, at least, is incited by offers of reward to the man who shall first discover us. Tonight we will break camp, and try to find a more suitable place to make a final stand against these

THE COWBOY OF RAMAPO VALLEY.

invaders of our mountain home." Turning to Cobus, he ordered him to attend to getting everything in readiness to move at sunset.

As soon as the sun disappeared behind Torne Mountain the cowboys left their old camping ground, and under the lead of Cobus and the chief proceeded through the mountains towards the east. They traveled until near midnight when Claudius called a halt and told them this was the place he had selected to make a final stand against their enemies.

The place was **well** adapted to stand a siege, as nature had made it almost impregnable. A rocky gorge of many feet in depth cut into the mountain on the east. On the south was a huge precipice, the walls of which rose nearly perpendicular from the base of the hill, while on the west was another deep valley, down which a mountain torrent leaped in foamy **rage.** Only on the north side was it unprotected by nature's own handiwork; but on that side the plateau extended back almost **as** far as the eye could reach and for a distance of more than **five** hundred **feet** there was scarcely a **tree or bush to obstruct their** view.

Enemies approaching from that direction would have to expose themselves to view for all that distance, which would give the garrison of this natural fortress opportunity to pour a withering fire into their ranks from behind a breastwork built across from gorge to chasm.

In this place the cowboys made their camp. There was ample room for tents and all the camp equipment and before another night's shadows had darkened the surrounding landscape, the fortifications were completed and everything in readiness to receive the enemy.

It was then, when all had been done that could be done to make the stronghold of the tories safe against almost any number that might attack it that they had time to think and meditate on what might happen in the near future; and Claudius, whose mind was ill at ease, was often in deep thought.

One day while they were still waiting to hear of the approach of the force they knew was being sent against them Cobus thus addressed his brother, who seemed to be in one of his melancholy moods:

"What ails you, Claudius? You seem to be in a gloomy state of mind these days, in fact so much so that our men have noticed it and it is having a bad effect upon them! They say your courage must be failing, and that you are brooding over expected defeat!"

"Cobus," replied the tory chief, "do you believe that one human being can look farther into the future than another?"

"Well," said Cobus, "I have heard that there are persons who can see into the future and tell to almost a certainty, what is to befall another; but I have had no experience in that line myself and do not place much confidence in such stories. But why do you ask me such a question, Claudius?"

"It was about the beginning of the war," replied his brother, "that I happened near Call Hollow (which you know is about midway between the Point of the Mountain and King's Ferry) and visited an old crone who resides there in a dilapidated old hut and got her to tell my fortune. And to tell you the truth, Cobus, thus far in my career, her words have come true! It was a terrible horoscope she drew for me and if the end should prove to be as she foretold then indeed am I doomed! It was a mere fit of curiosity which impelled me to call on her and I never took her prophecy seriously; but still, when I recognize the fact that a part of it has come true, I cannot help but feel a little anxious as to whether the other part of it may not be the same."

"Throw these gloomy forebodings from your mind and be yourself again! Much depends upon you in the coming struggle!" said Cobus.

"What you say is true and I will take your advice," replied the chief.

CHAPTER XXI.

Captain Rem. and his company of scouts were making a thorough search for the hiding place of the cowboys and had covered the ground from Verdrietige Hook to the Kakiatt Hills when one of his men came in and announced that he had found, (as he described it), "the nest of the cowboy gang." He described the place as **well** as he could to Rem. and said they were located on a point **of the** mountains that was almost impregnable by nature.

Captain Onderdonk and his brother Dirck knew **the** spot well and coincided with the report he brought as to its being one of the strongest natural fortresses in the whole Ramapo range. They knew that the only way to assault it successfully would be to attack the position with a large force from two directions at once.

Nothing had been heard from Barent and his

men yet, but Rem. supposed they must be within a very short distance of where the cowboys were stationed. After consulting with some of his officers, Captain Onderdonk sent a messenger to find Barent and his men, if possible, and invite him to a conference before the attack was made, so that they might have an understanding as to the manner in which it should be conducted.

The messenger returned the next day and reported that he had found them about three miles west of the tory stronghold and that Captain Van Houten would meet him at a point about half way between the two companies.

In accordance with this understanding the two commanders met a short distance from the base of the mountain and there laid out the plan of attack. The next morning after the conference they were to march toward one another and dispose their forces so as to surround the cowboy rendezvous as nearly as possible. Whichever company got into position first should notify the other by a single rifle shot.

It was toward evening the next day and Rem. and his men were making their way as well as they could over the rocks and through bushes along the Summit of the range, when, from toward the west, came the report of a single rifle ringing through the forest, notifying him that Barent and his men were in position. In a short time an answering report told Captain Van Houten that the scouts, too, were in their place.

The besiegers saw the difficulties which faced them and were pretty well satisfied that the only vulnerable point of the tory position was on the north side, and that to capture the place they must make the assault from that direction and carry it at the **point of** the bayonet. But even to attempt that **would** incur a heavy loss, and many of their men **who** had passed through the long and weary struggle which had about ended, safely, would now be laid low by the bullets of this outlawed band.

It was the intention of both commanders to capture or destroy these marauders with as little loss of life on their part **as** possible. But they were in **a** strong position, and to carry it, there must necessarily be some **sacrifices.**

The fight began almost immediately after the two companies got into position, and a continuous discharge of musketry was kept up until night closed in around the combatants. In the evening Captain Barent and his men met and determined on a plan of assault. This was that Barent and his company should keep up the fire from across the valley to the west, while Rem. and his command should clamber up the gorge on the east side, gain the plateau and just as morning dawned, charge the breastworks which covered the position of the cowboys on the north.

Toward midnight Captain Rem. led his men up through the rocky chasm as quietly as possible. Like beasts of prey stealing on their victims, the scouts crept over the many obstructions in their path, now crawling on their knees through the dense laurel bushes which grew along the precipitous sides of the gorge and again clambering over the rough and scraggy rocks that lined the bottom of the ravine. They finally reached the summit of the plateau about an hour before daybreak.

It was arranged that just as soon as it was light

enough to see at all, the company from Fort Sidman should begin firing and make as great a demonstration as possible, to attract the attention of the tories, while the scouts, under Captain Rem, should then charge the breastwork from the north. They therefore lay on their arms **waiting** for daybreak. They had gained the position without alarming the besieged, and were ready to rush upon the cowboys at a moment's notice.

Just as the first sign of daylight lit up the eastern sky a terrific discharge of fire arms greeted the tories **from** across the valley to the west. It was the signal for the scouts to charge the fortifications, and as the tories were in the act of returning the fire a shout was heard, and as they turned to find out from whence it came they saw the whole company with Captain Rem. at its head in the act of mounting the embankment.

"Come on, my men! Use only cold steel!" shouted their leader, as he sprang over the earth works, followed by his men.

The cowboys were in a measure surprised by the sudden onset, but still they were soon ready to receive them. Rem. raged through the fight like a demon and got so far in advance of his men that, at one time, he was completely surrounded by the desperate tories. But with every swing of his good right arm a cowboy bit the dust, and very soon he cleared a place around him.

"At them, boys!" cried he; "down with the abductors of women!"

"It was a bloody and terrible hand to hand struggle which now ensued. Man to man! face to face! they met, with all the accumulated hatred of years nerving each arm and inspiring every heart.

Captain Rem. hunted for the tory chief and at last saw him in the act of cutting down one of the scouts whose valor had urged him too far from his command. With one bound the giant scout was upon him!

"I have found you at last!" cried Rem, as he grasped the tory leader by the throat and hurled him to the ground. But Claudius, with one overpowering effort, struggled to his feet, and with intense hate flashing from his eyes, faced the scout. Both were armed with heavy swords, and as they fought, and with skill parried each other's blows, they unconsciously approached the precipice at the south side of the plateau. Captain Rem. was between it and the cowboy chief and just in time saw what Claudius meant. Rushing forward he grasped the tory's coat, and, with all the power of his strong arm, with a backward motion threw him over into the abyss! Not stopping to see what became of him, Rem. joined his men just as the last of the cowboys surrendered.

The whole band, except three, were either killed or prisoners. These three men, being near the breastwork, when they saw the folly of further resistance, sprang into the forest and made good their escape.

After the battle, Captain Rem. sent half a dozen men to bring in the body of the tory chief. After a long search they returned with the information that it was nowhere to be found. They saw where he had fallen on a ledge, not more than ten feet from the top ; and from the broken twigs and bushes below, they were sure he had escaped, after all, by climbing down the face of the mountain.

The destruction of the cowboy band was complete, even though their leader had for the present saved himself. This gang of marauders, who, for more than seven years had been the terror of the district, were dispersed and scattered so thoroughly that the prospect of their ever becoming the cause of trouble again to the inhabitants of this part of the country, was slight indeed.

After dismantling the fortifications erected by the cowboys and collecting the booty found in their stronghold, Captains Barent and Rem. repaired with their companies to Fort Sidman.

CHAPTER XXII.

From the surrender of Cornwallis to the third of September, 1783, when the treaty of peace was signed at Paris, the two armies lay inactive except that each held the forts and cities they occupied at the time. When the news came that the treaty had been signed by the representatives of the two nations and that Great Britain had recognized the Independence of the United States, the country put on its holiday garb and gave itself over to rejoicing, at this, the closing event of the long and sanguinary struggle for liberty.

It was not until the 25th day of November of the same year, that the British army evacuated the city of New York. As the last of the invaders embarked for England, Washington, at the head of his victorious army entered the city amid the acclamations of the citizens, who made it a day of **rejoicing and** thanks to Almighty God for the great deliverance.

Shortly afterward Washington repaired to Annapolis, where Congress was in session, and formally resigned his commission, accompanying his act with a short and affecting speech, in which he briefly enumerated the chief events of the war, and commended his country to the protection of Heaven.

This was the last act in the great and bloody drama which had ended in making a free people and establishing an asylum for the oppressed of all nations. Since then, from this western land has radiated the beneficent and invigorating warmth of this sun of liberty, whose rays still enlighten this glorious hemisphere where freedom had its birth place.

That Claudius had escaped safe and sound was believed by Rem, and he felt that his mind would never be at ease until that king of the cowboys and tories was brought to justice. It was known that the Smith family originally came from Long Island and thither Rem. felt sure the tory chief had fled. Cobus and two others of the band had also escaped just as the fight ended, and the general opinion was that they also were concealed at the same place.

As the war was now over and peace had been proclaimed throughout the land Rem. procured a warrant from a civil magistrate in which Claudius and his brother were charged with the murder of several citizens of the County of Orange. This was placed in the hands of an officer, who, accompanied by Rem. and Dirck, immediately proceeded to Long Island in search of the outlaws. They arrived there in due time, disguised as farm laborers who were looking for work among the farms of the Island. For some time they could hear nothing of the fugitives and began to think they had taken refuge in some other locality.

The part of the island where they were searching was mainly inhabited by royalists, whose sympathies were with the enemies of the country, which made it difficult to get any information that would lead to the arrest of the cowboys.

It was probably a week after their arrival before they got any knowledge of the hiding place of the fugitives. One day as Rem. was listlessly wandering about he thought he caught a glimpse of Claudius at a farm house near the little village of Huntington. He reported what he had discovered to Dirck and the officer and they determined to set a watch that night upon the premises.

As soon as twilight cast its uncertain shadows over the village they repaired to the place and secreted themselves where they could see any one who might enter or leave the suspected house. They had been concealed but a short time when the door opened and Claudius stepped out. He cast furtive glances to the right and left and then cautiously walked out upon the highway and started down the road past where Rem. and his party were concealed. He got just opposite to them, when all three sprung in front of him. He attempted to draw a pistol, but he was already covered by the weapons of his captors, and, upon the demand of the officer, surrendered without striking a blow.

The surprise was so complete and sudden that he had no chance to resist. He was immediately disarmed and shackled, and then placed in charge of Rem. and Dirck.

It was now Rem's opportunity to gloat over his fallen enemy, but his soul revolted at the thought. Our hero was made of different stuff, and in his heart he felt a certain commiseration for the conquered bandit.

The next object of the officer and his companions was to secure the other three men. They therefore took Claudius to the village jail where he could be kept safely until the others were captured. The attempt to get from the tory chief any information as to the place they were secreted in, of course was futile. He had too much honor left to divulge the place of their concealment and stubbornly refused to tell anything that might lead to their arrest.

They finally enlisted the services of the local officers of the law in their cause, and before a week transpired all three were captured.

The next object of the captors was to get their prisoners safely into Goshen jail. For that purpose, and to guard against any attempt their friends might make to rescue them, they raised a posse to accompany them on their journey home.

It was a long and dangerous road they had to

travel to reach their destination; but fortune favored them, and in five days from the time they started with their prisoners they arrived safe and sound at the county seat of Orange, and incarcerated this remnant of the cowboy band behind the bars of Goshen jail.

Here they remained for several weeks while the authorities were preparing for their prosecution by collecting all the evidence possible from the surrounding district. It was determined to give them a fair and impartial trial, and every advantage the law allowed to persons charged with crime.

At last the day arrived and Claudius and his men were arraigned at the bar of justice. When the question was put to them as to whether they were guilty or not guilty each man arose in his place and answered in the negative.

The trial proceeded and able counsel was employed to defend the cowboys and Claudius himself was active in their defense, often asking questions and suggesting others to their lawyers.

The case dragged along for many days and caused a great sensation throughout the whole county and even far beyond its limits. The Court House was packed with eager listeners each day. Men from the mountains, from Long Island, and members of the families, some one of whom had suffered from the ruthless actions of the band, were in attendance, anxious to see and note each phase of the drama being enacted before them.

Finally, the time came when the evidence both for and against was all in, and the counsel were ready to make their pleas to the jury who had patiently set for many days listening to the testimony.

The prosecution had succeeded in proving its case against all the prisoners at the bar and there was no doubt in the minds of the spectators as to their guilt. The jury retired, and, after deliberating for several hours, came into the court and returned a verdict of "guilty" against them all. The judge then arraigned them separately for sentence.

When Claudius was placed at the bar and the question was put to him whether he had anything to say why sentence of death should not be passed upon him he arose, and thus addressed the court :

"May it please your honor! I know that nothing
"I can say will avert the doom that awaits me;
"but it may be the last opportunity I shall have to
"excuse my past life before the people! I was
"born among these mountains and from youth
"until manhood I roamed over them, free and
"unshackled as the air I breathed! No word of
"dishonor was ever coupled with the name I bore
"and I looked forward to a life of respectability
"and usefulness!

"I had scarcely attained manhood when this
"war began, and, as everyone knows, I espoused
"the cause of the mother country! This
"was the one great and overwhelming fault—
"the greatest sin in the estimation of my enemies,
"which I could, under any circumstances have
"committed! But in my heart I thought I was
"doing right, and may your honor please, I have
"never repented that choice! I am still a tory,
"and your honor knows what that word signifies
"among the self-styled patriots of our land!

"Inasmuch as I espoused that cause I deemed it my duty to further the interests of my King in every way I could! I gathered around me a loyal band of fighters for the King and Parliament and did their enemies all the damage in my power!

"Though I **never** was enlisted **among** the British regulars I fought **my battles** with an honest heart and thought **I was** serving my country as well as they!

"I admit that I have been instrumental in putting men to death; but on every occasion it was in open fight or **in** the attempt to take from rebels to their King provisions needed by the adherents to our cause! For our opinion's sake both me and mine have been persecuted, but all through these cruel years I have still been steadfast to my first love!

"For this great crime I am about to die. But yet if I could live these years again, I would again be guilty of the same offence! If for the cause of liberty these same deeds had been done you would have called me patriotic and praised **these** 'deeds of blood' as you now term them and

"would have said to me, 'well done. thou good
"and faithful servant!'

"But why should I thus stand here and speak
"in vain? I know the fiat has gone forth and we
"must pay the penalty you have provided. But I
"have given you some wholesome truths and
"thank you for the opportunity! I do not whine
"and whimper at my fate nor with driveling tears
"supplicate for mercy. All I ask your honor for,
"is to let the day come quickly for our execution
"and that you do not keep us in suspense! I am
"ready for the ordeal and shall meet it like a
"soldier!

The other men made no remarks before their sentence. They were ordered to stand up, and the judge sentenced all to be hung at Goshen Jail on the 20th day of December, 1783.

When the day of fate came round Claudius and his companions were led out, and, between two ranks of the veteran scouts of Captain Rem, were marched to the gallows, which had been built a short distance from the jail and on the ground now comprising the village green of Goshen.

Around the scaffold in hollow square stood the

stern and war-worn veterans of the Revolutionary army. The local officers of the law were in attendance preparing the prisoners and adjusting the machinery of death.

Claudius and his brother retained their composure to the last. The towering form of the tory chief was erect and his mien as proud as when he stood at the head of his bandit followers.

Just before the signal was given to cut the cord, Claudius bade his fellow victims farewell and in a loud, strong voice, announced himself ready. The sheriff stepped back, and, at his signal, the executioner severed the cord that held the fatal trap door, and all that was left of the terrible band of marauders was launched into eternity.

Thus was the prophecy of the old crone of Call Hollow fulfilled, and in the death of Claudius the country was rid of a scourge, but who, under other circumstances, might have been one of the great ones of the land and an honor to his birthplace.

The bodies of the cowboys were buried in the old jail yard and in after years, when a new court house was being built, the laborers who were digging for the foundation exhumed four human skeletons which were recognized by some of the old inhabitants of Goshen as those of Claudius and his three men.

The bones of these skeletons were not immediately reinterred, but remained above ground until the court house walls were being built, when one of the masons took the skull of Claudius, which was known from its greater size, and built it into the front wall, immediately over the front door of the court house, where, in all probability, it remains to this day.

CHAPTER XXIII.

After the proclamation of peace and the disbanding of the Revolutionary army, the fortifications at Fort Sidman and other parts of Ramapo Pass were abandoned, and Captain Rem. and Barent returned to their respective homes. Throughout the long struggle they had filled their positions with honor to themselves and benefit to their country, and now, when they retired to rural pursuits, and to enjoy the blessings for which they had given the best years of their lives, they did so among a people who loved and respected them.

As years wore away, and the people began to realize, more and more, the great blessings to the country which the great conflict had insured, every actor in it was reverenced and loved as a benefactor of his race.

The long struggle, as is always the case, left the

country heavily in debt and the disbanding of the army threw a large number of men, who for years had known no other employment than that of the soldier, upon the communities of the different States. By their long service, many of them had become totally unfitted for the duties and functions of civil life and became wanderers and vagrants over the land.

The morality, also, of a nation suffers in consequence of war, especially in those portions where the army has been mainly located—for it is a well known fact that men will become more or less corrupt by the close and intimate association of great numbers. These disadvantages of course were not peculiar to the United States, neither was she excepted from this general rule and was bound to suffer accordingly.

We will now return to the rural scenes where our story began, and, with the reader, find out in what condition the war had left them.

The desolate appearance caused by the cowboy raid on the premises of old Martinus Onderdonk had disappeared, and in the place where the burned buildings had stood, new and substantial barns and outbuildings had been erected. The old man and his wife, on **account** of the weight of years, had in a measure **retired** from the management of the **farm,** and Rem. and Dirck and their only sister Katharine, had taken their places in **the** active work of conducting the place. Black George was still there, and as chief of the retainers, magnified his office, and felt that the whole management of the farm rested upon his shoulders.

Since the war ended Rem. had bent all his energy toward making the farm yield as much as possible and also in beautifying its surroundings, until now, two years after hostilities had ceased, it **not** only produced abundantly but was also a thing of beauty to the eye. The broad fields and verdant meadows stretched away almost as far as the eye could reach, covered with waving grain and luxuriant grass.

It was in this rich **and** fertile valley, also, that the farms **of** old Rulof Van Houten and Bernard Demaray were situated; and the three together formed what everyone admitted them to be, the garden of **the** county. Their productiveness was proverbial and the beauty of their location was the admiration of all the country round.

Barent **Van** Houten, **as** might have been expected, **was an** almost daily visitor at the Demaray homestead, **and in** the **society of Mary,** passed much of his **time.** When his company was disbanded he was accompanied home by Lieutenant Bertholf, his warm personal friend and companion throughout the whole conflict.

From some intimations already thrown out, the reader will surmise what attracted him thither, and will not be surprised at finding him spending many pleasant hours at the side of Miss Katharine and in the **enjoyment** of the hospitalities **of** the Onderdonk home.

At the earnest solicitations **of** Barent and Rem, he remained in the neighborhood several weeks and when at last, he left for his home beyond the mountains, he carried with him the self satisfying knowledge that he was the accepted lover of Katharine Onderdonk.

For Captain **Rem, the** world jogged along in the old groove. **From** the time he reached manhood he had been **a** soldier, with **no** time to waste on love or women; and now, when the tumultuous scenes of the struggle were past the old habits still stuck to him, and he settled down into calm and contented bachelorhood.

The care of the farm occupied a portion of his time, and when not engaged in that, he gave his attention to his books of which he had collected a library of all the best in science and history to be procured; and among them he found his greatest enjoyment.

But the time came when Captain Rem's fellow citizens, recognizing his ability and knowledge of the world, looked to him as the one above all in the district most competent to represent them in the councils of the nation, and he was almost unanimously elected as a Member of Congress. He performed the duties imposed upon him so well that he was returned again and again, until, as the years passed, it became a burden to him and he voluntarily retired to private life. When finally old age came, and bent him with its weight of years, he died as he had lived, surrounded by friends and respected by all who knew him.

Captain Barent Van Houten was instrumental in organizing the new State and became prominent in civil life as he had been in the troublous times that were past. It was to him, also, that the power was given to organize the militia of the county, and he was appointed the first commander and received his commission as Brigadier General from General George Clinton, the first Governor of the State.

When peace was fairly established and the machinery of civil government began to run smoothly, and such men as Captain Barent Van Houten and Rembrandt Onderdonk were elevated to places of power and honor, then the people settled down with the assurance that every man would receive the protection he was entitled to by law and for the first time came over them that feeling of security which had been interrupted for eight long years of turmoil and uncertainty.

It was a lovely summer morning in the month of June, 1785, that the wedding bells rang out from the old Dutch Church at Tappan, and from the surrounding country the people were congregating to witness a double wedding. The two couples who were about to enter the domain of Hymen, were representatives of the leading families of the County of Orange and loved and respected by all.

Captain Barent Van Houten, and the lovely Mary Demaray ; and Lieutenant Henry Bertholf, and the beautiful and accomplished Katharine Onderdonk were to be married that morning and the whole congregation of the church was coming out to witness the ceremony.

When the hour arrived the good old Dominie Demaray—a near relative of Mary—came down the aisle, the bridal party arranged themselves facing the preacher's desk, and when, after an hour's service—for it took a good while to get married in those days—the white-haired minister pronounced them wedded the vast assemblage congratulated them and wished them joy and all the blessings of a long and prosperous life.

Thus were they wedded in the midst of friends and neighbors and through their long and useful lives they never regretted the day that made them one; and in after years when sons and daughters were born and grew up around them they blessed that day again and never forgot to make it a day of rejoicing while they lived.

www.ingramcontent.com/pod-product-compliance
Lightning Source LLC
Chambersburg PA
CBHW020912230426
43666CB00008B/1424